She Was God's *Masterpiece*

She Was God's Masterpiece

Copyright © 2010 by Joel E. Reed, M.D.

Published by Lucid Books in Brenham, TX.
    www.LucidBooks.net

All rights reserved. No part of this publication may be reproduced, stored in a retrieval system, or transmitted in any form by any means, electronic, mechanical, photocopy, recording, or otherwise, without the prior permission of the publisher, except as provided for by USA copyright law.

First Printing 2010

All Scripture quotations are from
Life Application Bible, New International Version
Published by Tyndale House Publishers, Inc. of Wheaton, Illinois and Zonderman Publishing House of Grand Rapids, Michigan.

ISBN-13: 978-0-9789265-8-8
ISBN-10: 0-9789265-8-7

Special Sales: Most Lucid Books titles are available in special quantity discounts. Custom imprinting or excerpting can also be done to fit special needs. Contact Lucid Books at info@lucidbooks.net.

She Was God's Masterpiece

JOEL E. REED, MD

LUCIDBOOKS

Dedication

Dedicated to the memory of Jeanne, my special angel, superwoman, wonder woman, and perfect wife. My best friend, God's masterpiece, and to all the family members who contributed their perspectives of this remarkable woman.

Acknowledgment

I want to acknowledge the invaluable help of my editor, Leigh McLeroy, whose business is appropriately named "Words that Work." She knew just how to pick the words to clarify what I wanted to say; and my close friend, Fred Korge, who led me to her and who has not only encouraged me but helped me make this into a real book.

Contents

Introduction. 1

1   A Death Sentence 5
2   The Early Years 11
3   A Fine Romance. 23
4   The Wedding 31
5   First Year of Marriage. 37
6   Finishing School 43
7   The Air Force Years. 51
8   Finally, Private Practice 83
9   Laughter Really Is The Best Medicine. . . 93
10   Jeanne 113
11   Boom Town Bust Causes Health Care Crisis. 125
12   God and Faith 131
13   Parenting. 163
14   Retirement. 177
15   Travel. 187
16   Ninety Days 205

Epilogue 221

Introduction

Rice University has a very fine continuing education program which is designed for the community at large and held at convenient evening hours. I had taken an intergenerational course in anthropology with my grandson Eric which was not only educational but fun and a great bonding experience for us. Having taken that course, I was, of course, on their mailing list for further course offerings. One that caught both Jeanne's and my attention was a course on genealogy.

My maternal aunt Ethel had searched the Woodward clan all the way back to 1750. She did it the hard way: visiting towns, scouring newspaper archives, and searching through graveyards reading the grave markers. Her aim was to get back far enough to qualify for membership in the Daughters of the American Revolution (DAR). Her search revealed many names in several generations. She did not need to go further because she had succeeded in showing that the clan had been here in the US since before the Revolutionary war. She had given me a copy of the book which had been on the bookshelf for many years.

The genealogy course at Rice University seemed to offer the chance to get more information than just a list of names, showing us how to search for wills, deeds to property, licenses, obituaries, and other documents which would give us an insight into who these relatives really were. We began a search for Jeanne's ancestors with some success. We even went to Salt Lake City to visit the Mormon Library. Their kind and patient volunteers were very helpful, sharing their expertise with us. We obtained much information about her ancestors, even the name of the ship upon which they sailed to the new world. But I hit a roadblock with mine. My paternal great grandparents had moved to Iowa from Schuylkill County, Pennsylvania and records prior to 1850 had been destroyed in a fire. I was never able to get information beyond that.

We decided that it might be meaningful to subsequent generations of our family to leave a record of our lives. We wanted them to know who we really were. What were our lives like? We wanted them to know about our occupations, hopes, fears, faith, etc.—in other words, what made us tick.

Then the opportunity arose. The Retired Physicians Organization to which we both belonged sponsored a class called Life Writing which is still being given after several years. It focused more on the ways to write than on what we felt was helpful to us in getting started and organized for a personal family history. We were taught how to write in the third person, how to write poetry, keep a journal, write personal letters, etc. I always felt correctly or not, that anything I wrote would have to be my style. It needed to reflect me and my personality.

We both wrote a few vignettes in class, but could never get going with the full story as we wanted to tell it. Jeanne's recent death made it clear to me that I must get to work if it was ever to get done. The following is the result of that effort.

1
A Death Sentence

For several years routine checkups had revealed that Jeanne had intermittent and very slight elevations of a liver enzyme. She experienced no symptoms suggestive of liver disease and various explanations for the enzyme elevation were offered by different specialists. Finally her doctor recommended a needle biopsy of the liver, but even its results were inconclusive, although a diagnosis of autoimmune hepatitis was proposed. Then a new blood test became available and Hepatitis C was diagnosed—something we felt that she might have contracted from a blood transfusion in 1963, or perhaps from immune globulin injections she received in the early 1970's. The only medicine with a chance of clearing the virus was a fairly toxic combination of Interferon combined with Ribavirin, but her condition seemed stable so we were advised to continue regular checkups and observation, awaiting potential new and more tolerable treatments.

Then an acute flare up occurred, with worsening laboratory tests and increased weakness. We made the rounds of several specialists both in Houston and Dallas, but none could explain the sudden change. We even traveled to the Mayo clinic for a week-long comprehensive evaluation, where they ran every possible test but could offer no explanation for the change. Her condition was stabilizing with few symptoms and close observation was again the course of action advised.

Feeling somewhat desperate we decided to try the interferon on reduced dosage to see how well she could tolerate it, but even at lowered doses it made her feel terrible, with low grade fever, fatigue, aching and depression. The treatment seemed worse than the disease and even without it, her condition again stabilized with very few symptoms.

But there would be a change. In September 2006 vague and general symptoms developed and an ultrasound was done of the liver—but it showed no change from the previous test. Despite that fact and because of the symptoms, and a slight elevation of a laboratory test called AFP (alpha-fetoprotein), an MRI was ordered. Already two weeks had passed since we first saw the hepatologist and two more weeks went by before the MRI could be scheduled and performed. Days later we received a call that the doctor would like to see Jeanne and discuss the results. This I interpreted as a bad sign, since test results were usually reported on a form with a check mark by normal or a brief comment if abnormal, but stable.

A Death Sentence

Dr. Ankoma-Sey was a very kind and gentle physician to whom I had already given the highest compliment I ever give a fellow physician: he was an "old fashioned doctor." He sat across from us and told us that the tests confirmed the presence of liver cancer. Hearing that word, cancer, always evokes the response "death." It certainly did so that day for us. In spite of the advances in treating some types of cancer, we both knew that there was really no effective treatment of liver cancer short of transplantation. Yes, there were procedures that slowed its growth, even causing some tumor shrinkage, but no cure. He wanted to refer Jeanne to the transplant team at Baylor Medical School, and it is customary when a referral is warranted to give the patient a list of names from which they should choose. (Before the crazy law called HIPPA, a doctor would simply choose the person he felt was most qualified for the particular problem, call him to discuss the patient, and ask for specific recommendations.)

Following protocol, Dr. Ankoma-Sey offered us a list of three names. I told him that I would prefer to know who he would refer his own wife to in a similar situation. He then named Dr. John A. Goss, a surgeon, who headed the transplant team. To lessen the tension, I asked "Well, how do you get along with your wife?" After we all shared a laugh, this old fashioned doctor pulled out his cell phone and called Dr. Goss' office, only to learn that he was out of town at a medical meeting. No problem; he then dialed the doctor's cell phone and called him in San Antonio, reaching him right away. He explained the problem and we were told to be in Dr. Goss' office at 9:00AM the next day.

Dr. Goss went over Jeanne's test results and confirmed Dr. Ankoma-sey's diagnosis. He ruled out transplant because of Jeanne's age (81), stating that the operative risk was far too high especially in view of her complicating medical conditions, asthma and arteriosclerosis. He felt that the quality of life would be terrible as older patients did not tolerate the anti-rejection medications as well as younger ones did. He advised chemo-embolization instead, a procedure in which a catheter is threaded through the femoral artery (groin), up to the hepatic artery (liver) and even out to the specific location of the tumor. Then a chemotherapy drug is injected, immediately followed by an injection of suspended particles of albumen to block the blood supply to the region.

This treatment is designed to kill the tumor or at least set it back for awhile, and it is usually used to buy time till transplantation can be performed. After still another review of her case by an old friend, an oncologist who confirmed the diagnosis and concurred in the treatment plan, we decide to follow this approach.

By then, the Christmas holidays were upon us and we delayed the treatment till January after we were assured the delay would not change the ultimate result. Jeanne tolerated the chemo about as well as one can, suffering the usual hair loss, poor appetite and weight loss. Then the battle began to buy as much time as possible, and to crowd in all the joys she could in the short time she expected. Details of that battle and the happy times we shared, I will save for a later chapter. First I want to tell some of the stories of a family led by this remarkable lady whose nickname was "God's Masterpiece."

2

The Early Years

There were sharp contrasts between Jeanne's childhood and mine –but somehow our differences made us right for each other.

JOEL
   Actually, I have few memories of my early years—so few that I wonder if they might have been suppressed. I don't recall ever feeling poor or unhappy, but I know that times were hard. The Great Depression began when I was only four and the economy did not recover until after World War II. But recently, another man's memories of that time stirred some of my own.
   My niece Jane Kunzie-Brunner, a Lutheran Pastor in Lake Barrington, Illinois, asked me to read a book with the unusual title "A Nickel's Worth of Skim Milk." She planned to use some of it in a series of sermons on stewardship. The book's author, Robert J. Hastings, is just one year older than me and he characterized his book as "A Boy's View of the Great Depression." While our circumstances were quite different (he was raised

in a small town in southern Illinois surrounded by a large family and I was raised in large cities with only my mother nearby) we viewed the depression from the same age perspective and his story brought back many memories of my own.

I can recall spending a summer on a chicken ranch just outside Los Angeles with friends of my mother. At this farm I collected eggs, weighing them on a small balance scale to sort them as small or large. An egg that did not tip the scale was small. If it tipped the scale it was large, and if it could tip the scale with a hook weight attached it was an extra large jokingly called a "hooker". The eggs were sold in town to regular customers. In addition to the sorting, I cleaned pens, and (rarely) chopped the head off of a fryer and picked the feathers. I also tended a garden in which there were many vegetables.

In town, during school months, I had a number of jobs even before my teen years. I mowed a neighbor's lawn for 25 cents, worked in a furniture store on Saturdays for 10 cents an hour, dusting and touching up wood scratches with a crayon. I delivered the Saturday Evening Post for pennies a copy and placed ads on door handles, also for pennies. For a while I worked as a soda jerk in an ice cream store, also earning 10 cents an hour plus all the ice cream I could hold. My best job came when I was 15, working in a neighborhood "Red and White" grocery store stocking shelves, taking and delivering phone orders, sweeping up and occasionally helping the butcher. I might have done the same thing even had there not been a depression. I could use the money I earned for treats such as the Saturday movie, with its serials filmed to leave you in suspense waiting for next Saturday. Hastings' memories of the radio shows of the time were the same as mine. I honestly think that using our imagination to visualize the stories and the characters was better than viewing them on television.

There was never a time when I did not have plenty to eat and always had a roof over my head. Everyone seemed to be in the same circumstances so it all seemed normal. Of course, I heard about the WPA, CCC, and other government programs, but I don't remember knowing anyone who held one of those jobs.

My parents divorced when I was very young and I have no recollection of my father from those early years. My mother never discussed the reasons behind the divorce and I was too young to question or to understand. We moved frequently as my mother found various jobs. I can recall two of them, one as a church secretary and another as receptionist in a doctor's office. This was probably where I first decided that I wanted to be a doctor. My mother could take dictation by shorthand as fast as one could talk and was able to type almost as fast. With those skills, she always had a job, even though we moved often.

Because of those frequent moves, I attended many schools, some for only a year. The result was that I had no close friends, and with my extended family on both sides scattered in several states, I had virtually no contact with them as I grew up, either. It was just my mother and me.

Mother remarried when I was about 12 to a salesman whose work took us to San Jose for less than a year, San Francisco for a year, Des Moines, Iowa, for another year and finally to Minneapolis. Each move meant another new school. I remember little of my step-father except that I never felt close to him. He and my mother divorced the year we were in Minneapolis and she and I moved to Omaha, Nebraska, where mother's sisters Florence and Ethel lived. We lived only a couple blocks away from them in a small apartment.

World War II was in full swing in Europe and in the Far East then, but the attack on Pearl Harbor had not yet occurred. Our defense industries were producing at maximum capacity for the Lend-Lease program and mother got a job with a defense contractor as a typist but they had more typists than they really needed and mother could not sit still. She said that she spent a lot of time keeping her skills sharpened by typing over and over, "The quick brown fox jumped over the lazy dog." This sentence contained most of the letters of the alphabet and kept her proficient.

We were having our Sunday dinner, early on the afternoon of December 7, 1941, when we heard on the radio that Pearl Harbor was under attack. The next day Congress declared war on Japan. I was 16 years old and a junior in high school. By taking extra credits, I was able to graduate a semester early, in December 1942. The summer before my senior year mother married Harry Wilson, a railroad conductor and moved to

Hastings, Nebraska. Since my graduation was only a couple of months away, I convinced them that I should stay in Omaha at Aunt Florence's so that I would not have to change schools.

Harry was a fine and caring person and I came to respect and love him though we never spent a lot of time together because of my school, and then later the military service.

My high school grades had been high enough to win a full scholarship to Omaha University (now University of Nebraska, Omaha Division). Shortly after the start of college in January 1943, I was given the opportunity to join the College Naval Reserve. It promised completion of one year (two accelerated semesters) in Omaha, then, on to the Navy Officers Training School ("90 day wonders") and enlistment as an Ensign. I needed my mother's permission as I was still only 17 years old, but everyone supported the war and she willingly agreed.

Before the first semester was over, the Navy changed me from college reserve to a program called V-12. I was placed on active duty and ordered to a college of the Navy's choice, Ursinus College, Collegeville, Pennsylvania. I had never heard of the school until I received those orders. I did find it in the encyclopedia and learned that it was a fine small college near Philadelphia. It was especially known for its pre-med program.

Two-hundred of us V-12s arrived at Ursinus on June 1, 1943, from all over the country, and were immediately issued Navy uniforms, I.D. cards, and assigned four to a dorm room. There was a Navy Lieutenant as Commander, an Ensign as adjutant, and a Chief Petty Officer, all of whom did their best to make this a mini-academy. There was also a corpsman who did our physicals and treated minor illnesses. We were subject to Navy discipline, being awakened by bugle call at 6:00 AM to run a mile, shower, dress in our uniforms, make up our rooms for inspection, "fall in" for roll call and personal inspection, march to raising the colors, and finally march to the "mess hall" for breakfast. We were then free to attend classes which always started at 8:00 AM.

For most, the classes were general liberal arts courses with a couple of Navy classes such as naval organization and naval science and tactics. Many of my fellow students took German though I do not remember if it was a requirement. To my delight, there were a couple of openings in the pre-medical course and I was fortunate to be picked for one of them. Medicine had always been a dream of mine but we did not have the resources for me to even seriously consider it. The Navy made it possible. That also meant that I would stay at Ursinus until I met the requirements to enter medical school. Since we were all on a wartime accelerated program (three semesters a year), by taking heavy loads (as many as 21 hours a semester) I was able to graduate with a Bachelor of Science degree by June 1945, at 19 years of age.

While awaiting entry into medical school, I was assigned as a corpsman to the Naval Hospital, Bainbridge, Maryland. The war ended that summer, but I was still sent to Northwestern University Medical School (one of the finest in the country) and completed one semester before being discharged by the Navy. On top of all that good fortune, I was eligible for 16 months more of school under the G.I. Bill of Rights. My final semesters were subsidized by my fraternal Aunt Myra Root and by multiple part time jobs. It was during my sophomore year that I met Jeanne.

JEANNE

Jeanne's childhood was quite different from mine. I would call it idyllic. Her sister, Caryl, characterized it as "wonderful."

Jeanne was surrounded by multiple generations of a big family. Her maternal Great Grandfather, Christian Jung, emigrated to the U.S. in June 1882 from a small town in southern Germany, Offenbach am Glan. With him were his wife Elizabeth Von Post, his widowed father Karl, and siblings Dorothea, Louisa, Charlotte and George. Four children, Charles Jung (also known as Carl and nicknamed Bobo by the great-grandchildren), Louise, Bertha, and Louis also came over on the same ship, the Belgenland, which was a four masted sailing vessel with one steam engine. They travelled steerage class, landing in New York on June 9, 1882. Two more children were born to Christian and Elizabeth in the US, daughters Sophie and Emma. Distant relatives lived in the Chicago area so they settled there. There were frequent family get togethers as it was a close knit family. Carl (Charles) married Augusta ("Gussie") and had four children, Edna Louise (Jeanne's and Caryl's mother), Carl Ludwig, and twins Elsa Sophie and Irene Lucy. Irene Lucy died shortly after birth.

Three generations lived in the middle class home at 8132 South Ada Street in Chicago: Carl and Augusta, Edna and her husband Robert Vogel and their two children, Jeanne and Caryl. For awhile even Robert's mother lived with them. They moved into this house when Jeanne was four years old and Caryl was four months old. Jeanne and Caryl shared a bedroom and the sisters were very close. If there were any problems they were related to the fact that there was only one bathroom.

Caryl remembers no conflicts with Jeanne, nor did they ever fight. Caryl remarked that "Jeanne was always there for me." The two communicated freely and Caryl could recall long conversations, some lasting till the wee morning hours. They walked to elementary school together even before Caryl was old enough to enroll; in those days it was safe for children to walk in their neighborhood. Jeanne's high school was also within walking distance. She was together with many of her classmates throughout elementary and high school and developed lifelong friendships with them.

Robert "Bob" Vogel (Jeanne's father) was somewhat stiff and controlling, and not intimately involved with the children's daily lives. He was a purchasing agent at Chicago meat packer Swift & Company and remained employed throughout the Great Depression. As a father he always seemed to want more from the girls even when they did well. Jeanne was obedient and willing to go with the flow. She was not a doormat but was never encouraged to be assertive. She was a strong student with excellent grades and aspired to go to Stanford and regretted not doing so. (I am forever grateful that she didn't or I probably would not have met her.) Bob pushed her to go into nurses training, specifically into the Cadet Nurse Corps, sponsored by the Army with the requirement that she would enter the Army as a nurse upon completion of her training. (The war ended before that became necessary.) Jeanne later admitted that she might have come to the same conclusion, but wanted to make the decision on her own. Her father bragged that he "got her in" to the Wesley Hospital, Northwestern University program because of his friendship with Mr. Holmes who was on the board of Swift & Co. The truth is, her grades were good enough for her to go wherever she wished.

One of her dreams was to become an airline stewardess which, in those days, required that one be a nurse. Nursing school meant taking classes during the day and then working in the hospital on the 3:00 PM to 11:00 PM shift under supervision of a registered nurse, routine that eventually led to a diploma and licensure as a Registered Nurse.

Jeanne always felt that the diploma program which led to status as a registered nurse was somewhat less prestigious than a college degree. She later made an attempt to take the remaining courses leading to a degree by distance learning. We were living in Indianapolis where I was taking my residency training in internal medicine. Though this was 1952, Butler University was already pioneering televised courses. By that time, however, we had two small children and the distractions were too much for her to be able to concentrate on the classes. The children vying for attention took priority over watching a class on TV. When we settled in Houston some years later, she went to Texas Women's University in the Texas Medical Center to enroll but they would not accept her credits from Northwestern because too much time had elapsed. She would have had to go a full four years.

I regret terribly that I did not realize how much it meant to her to get that degree, for we could have made it possible. To me it would have been symbolic only, because I always felt that she was the smartest woman with the quickest mind that I ever knew. She enriched her mind by reading many, many books. A degree would not have changed that. She was such a wonderful psychologist that I told her, "If you had gone to medical school, you would have been either the greatest pediatrician or psychiatrist of all time. Freud and Jung would look like amateurs."

Jeanne also exhibited musical talent. Her piano playing was good enough that she accompanied the girls' choir at Calumet High school and she also had a good voice and sung in the Gilbert & Sullivan operetta "The Mikado" in 6th grade as one of the "three little girl are we."

Despite the pressure to excel Jeanne had an excellent relationship with her parents, but her real love was her maternal grandfather Carl, or "Bobo", the nickname given to him by his first great grandchild Caryl. Jeanne and her sister Caryl called him Grandpa and daughter Edna called him PaPa. He was an especially loving person, kind, caring and non-judgmental. These characteristics were clearly inherited by Jeanne and were recognized by all who knew her.

The family owned a cabin near Pullman, Michigan, on Scott Lake. It was their escape from the crowded city of Chicago. Jeanne loved to swim and this love of the water lasted all her life. When the cabin was sold, Bobo and Gussie (called More Grandma by the grandchildren) would drive to St. Petersburg, Florida every year. Jeanne would always be in tears when they left. She was very close to them and had a strong bond. One year when Jeanne was 15 and Caryl 11, they travelled unaccompanied from Chicago to Florida by train. This was quite an accomplishment for two so young.

Jeanne and I met while she was a senior nursing student and I was a sophomore medical student and, from the moment I met her, I could think of no one else.

3

A Fine Romance

College was relatively easy for me, at least the courses in scientific subjects. I had expected medical school to be much the same and was somewhat surprised when I learned that this was going to be real work. There was so much to be studied in depth, so much to understand fully and to store in memory. We all studied until late at night or into the early morning hours whenever there was a test, which was almost daily.

An example was one of my first courses, embryology, which I had taken in college using the textbook written by Dr. Leslie B. Arey. Dr. Arey was the Embryology Professor at Northwestern and taught the course there. Since I had already taken the course in college using his own textbook and receiving an A grade, I was sure this would be easy. I did not plan to spend much time studying this course. Surprise! Dr. Arey went so far beyond the text and taught in such depth that I felt lucky when I got a B- on my first test. I determined I wouldn't let that happen again.

What little time I had was spent on various part time jobs to make a little money as I was quite poor. Selling blood to the blood bank was a quick source of cash but there was always a limit on the frequency of donations. Other means of income included writing histories and physicals on evening admissions to neighborhood hospitals, filing charts at Wesley Hospital, working as a night hotel clerk (at the Lawson YMCA), and the best one of all, working in the emergency room of Ravenswood hospital which paid full room, board and laundry for working one night in three. Each of these jobs allowed time for study.

I had little time for dating, plus I had a girlfriend back home in Nebraska. Our relationship was not serious but looked like it might become so when we had more time together.

Like most medical students of that time, I joined a fraternity for the fellowship and for a sort of family away from home. My fraternity (Phi Rho Sigma) was holding a formal dance and I did not plan to attend. One of my fraternity brothers was pushing me to get a date and go to the dance. I pleaded that I wasn't feeling completely over a case of viral pneumonia but the main reason was the cost of renting a tux, buying a corsage and paying for a taxi. He persisted, telling me that I must meet this girl (Jeanne) as she "was really something special." (He knew her because he was dating her roommate.) At his urging, the four of us met for a casual lunch at the hospital cafeteria. She completely blew me away with her beauty and intelligence, and she was (and would remain) the best conversationalist I had ever known. I felt more comfortable with her than any girl I had ever met and could hardly wait until the next day to call her and ask her to go to the dance. She later admitted to me that she was anxiously waiting for my call. If there is such a thing as love at first sight, this was it. I was able to sell a pint of blood to help finance the expense of the dance. Blood was purchased by the blood banks in those days for $25 a pint, and that was a fortune.

I think we dated every day or evening from that day forward. Jeanne spent her days in nursing classes then worked on the nursing units of the hospital from afternoon to late evening. By the time she finished her charting and gave report to the late shift, it would be 11:30 to 11:45 PM. I was still studying but would interrupt my studies and wait for her to get off work. She had to be in the nurse's quarters before midnight so our "date" was the walk from the hospital to the nurse's residence four blocks away. As our romance blossomed, the house mother would allow me to come in and let us sit in the card room for a short while after curfew.

We met on February 22, 1947. I was in my second semester as a sophomore medical student and Jeanne was a senior due to graduate in May. We fell in love so fast that I gave her my fraternity pin on her birthday, April 8, only 48 days after we met. (This was a sort of pre-engagement thing.) For her birthday, I took her out to dinner at a fancy steak house on Rush Street. I had saved up enough money - or so I thought. As soon as we were seated and I looked at the menu, I realized that, unless Jeanne ordered the cheapest thing on the menu (Salisbury steak—fancy talk for a hamburger patty!) I would have to plead that I didn't feel well and could only take a small cup of soup. The understanding and sensitivity that characterized her throughout her life showed when she did order the Salisbury steak. Even so, when the waiter brought the bill, I had only ten cents for a tip. He asked if I didn't want to give him something for his service. My response was "you've got it."

By the 18th of June (116 days from the date we met), I was able to tell her how very much in love with her I was, and ask her to marry me. It was not a very romantic setting; we were on the steps of the old armory which was across the street from the medical school and hospital, a spot along one of our walks to the nurses' residence. (That building has since been replaced by an art museum.)

I had wanted to ask her sooner but was afraid that she would feel that I was rushing things. It turned out my timing was right as she accepted immediately. Her only reservation was her asthma; she feared that it would be a problem. After I reassured her that I wanted to marry her "in sickness and in health," her fears quickly disappeared.

It wasn't long before the asthma did become an obstacle, however. Her allergist and her internist both recommended that she spend a year in Tucson where she would be away from the flora and fauna of northern Illinois and the airborne pollens and dusts that were suspected to be the cause. Though we hated the idea of being apart, we both knew that this was a wise approach since we had few options to control her disease.

When Jeanne left for Tucson, the plan was for her to stay there for one year to fully evaluate the effect on her asthma of Tucson's dry, warm, almost pollen- and organic dust-free atmosphere. Jeanne was experiencing continuous asthma at a level where she could function with difficulty and acute exacerbations that were so severe as to be life threatening. She had the finest doctors at Northwestern and had undergone extensive testing for allergen triggers and the best therapy available. Unfortunately, asthma was poorly understood in those days and therapy consisted of adrenalin by injection and aminophyllin (later discredited as relatively ineffective) both orally and by IV infusion, oxygen and the new ACTH, adrenocortical stimulation, and almost experimental, cortisone. Attacks required hospitalization in an oxygen tent and aggressive use of the above medicines. It could take several days of treatment just to get back to the chronic state.

Jeanne was to stay with a couple of elderly ladies and receive medical care from allergy specialists there. I was to continue school, starting my junior year. This year was centered on clinical care and there were fewer classes. There was, however, a large amount of reading and intense study. I was in misery. I missed Jeanne so much that I had trouble concentrating on my studies. I kept up reasonable grades but was very unhappy and the grades were falling. We wrote to each other daily but she was not improving and I was worrying more and more. Jeanne planned to work as an RN as soon as she passed the exam for licensure. It was a comprehensive exam covering the basic sciences and clinical care. True to form, Jeanne scored the second highest grade in the state on her exam and received a letter of commendation from the Licensure board. She started work in Tuscon but within a short time she developed pneumonia and was hospitalized. Her parents went to see her and returned to Chicago as soon as she improved. She was unable to return to work because the asthma was too severe, having been aggravated by the infection.

I finally decided that I must take leave of absence from school and go to Arizona to take care of her. I wanted to get married there, and if the climate change worked to help her asthma, I would try to transfer to a southwestern medical school. If this was not possible, after a reasonable trial period I would return to Northwestern if they would accept me back. I talked to the dean who strongly advised me not to leave school and insisted that I talk to the chief of medicine and psychiatry before making any final decision. I guess that he didn't realize that I felt she was far more important to me than medical school. As we both already knew, all the advisors said that I should remain in school.

I told the dean how strongly I felt and that I had firmly decided to leave at the end of the semester. I asked him if I could return if the climate change did no good and he promised me that there would be a place for me. I then asked if I could count on his help getting accepted at a southwestern medical school if the climate made a significant difference in the course of her asthma. He also agreed to that. So I began making plans to go to Arizona as soon as exams for the semester were over to face an uncertain future - but one with the girl I loved more than anything else at my side.

4

The Wedding

The last exam of the semester was on December 23, and I could not get a reservation to Tucson on that day or for that matter until after the Christmas season. I *could* get one to Phoenix on the 27th. That seemed close enough that I could get on a bus or train or even hitchhike to Tucson if necessary. I told Jeanne about the uncertainty and she sent me, by return mail, a ticket on Southern Arizona Airways from Phoenix to Tucson. It cost $19.95, a small fortune to us.

The flight to Phoenix was uneventful but arrived a little late. I rushed off of the plane at Phoenix and almost ran into the terminal as the connection allowed very little time. I couldn't find the check in counter for Southern Arizona Airlines and went to the American Airline Agent for help. She replied that she had not heard of Southern Arizona Airlines and knew for sure that they did not have a counter in the airport. She went further and consulted the telephone book and informed me that they were not listed! I was sure that Jeanne had been cheated by a con man and began to look for another way to Tucson. Shortly after, a man came up to me and asked if I were Mr. Reed. I replied that I was and he introduced himself to me, informing me that he was one of the owners of the airline. Southern Arizona Airlines was two air corps pilots from World War II who were trying to establish a shuttle service between Phoenix and Tucson. Unfortunately, the Cessna which they usually flew was in the shop. He offered on the spot to refund my fare and drive me to either the bus or train depot in his jeep. Seeing that I was clearly disappointed, he then told me that he owned an Aircoupe, a small single engine aircraft that looked like a WWII fighter plane, and that he would be glad to take me over to Tucson in it if I were game. I had never been in a small plane but was delighted at the chance to get to Jeanne quickly.

This was a plane first built just before WWII, with production restarted right after the war. There was barely room for the two of us in the seats and room for one suitcase behind the seats. There was a plastic canopy over the cockpit and a twin boom tail, no rudder pedals and a steering wheel which controlled both the rudder and the ailerons. We got in the plane and the pilot turned the ignition key. A big cloud of smoke came from under the cowling. He opened the canopy and said "run!" I ran one way and he another. He grabbed a fire extinguished and opened the cowling. There was no more smoke and he said it was not important as it had only been a bit of oil on the surface of the engine. "Was I still game," he asked? I thought with his experience as a pilot, if he thought it was OK so did I.

We got back in and he taxied to the end of the runway, instructing me to watch the tower for a green light which was the signal that we could go. Then he informed me that the only instruments aboard were a compass, an altimeter and an airspeed indicator. The green light flashed and he pushed the accelerator and told me "Go ahead and fly it." I told him that I had never flown before but he insisted, saying it was as easy as driving a car. "Just steer it in the center of the runway and when the airspeed indicator shows 60 mph, ease back on the steering wheel." I did just as he said and, indeed, it was easy. He told me the heading and not only let me fly it to Tucson but talked me through the landing. It was a bit bumpy for a landing but he told me that any landing that you walk away from is a good landing. He offered to give me flying lessons for just the cost of the gas which he estimated to be about $4.00 per hour. As enticing as that sounded, I still could not afford it. But it was a flight to remember.

Of course, Jeanne was not there waiting as we had landed on a small dirt strip on the edge of town. The pilot had anticipated this and told me she was probably at the big airport (Davis Monthan) looking for us. He drove me there, and there she was. It was a most joyful reunion.

Jeanne had already taken possession of the apartment which was to be our first home. It was a garage apartment behind the house at 1481 west 10th street. The owner had divided the garage in half with a shared bathroom. Quite adequate for a college student but even to us, it looked fine.

Jeanne's sister, Caryl, had already flown down to be maid of honor and a fraternity brother of mine, Randy Holmes, who lived in Phoenix, was my best man. Our wedding was to take place on the 29th of December, 1947.

Jeanne had made friends with a Missouri Synod Lutheran pastor who served the Indian reservation just outside of Phoenix, and he agreed to marry us in the chapel of the Methodist Church right across the street from the University of Arizona campus.

Jeanne wore a beautiful fitted grey suit she had bought previously on Michigan Avenue, with hat to match, and a pink silk blouse. She carried a family Bible covered in white silk, with a white orchid and trailing ribbons on top. She was breathtakingly beautiful. I always felt guilty that she did not get the formal church wedding with all the trimmings in Chicago where all her family and friends could attend, but she reassured me that she was very happy with the arrangements as they were.

After the ceremony, we went to the home of the ladies Jeanne had been staying with for wedding cake. The statue on the cake has been a part of all our children's weddings and of our two grandchildren who have already married. Our honeymoon was two nights in Tucson's Frontier Hotel, a gift from her parents. But that's all I will tell. The rest is censored.

The Wedding

Thus began one of the greatest love affairs ever—one which was to last over 60 years. I don't believe that there have ever been two people as passionately and deeply in love and as committed to each other as we were. I have prayed repeatedly that our children and their children will find such a love, as I have learned that true love like this is precisely the kind Paul describes in his letter to the Corinthians, and it is the most important thing in life. If you have never read or can't remember Paul's words, they are as follows:

"I may be able to speak the languages of men and even of angels, but if I have no love, my speech is no more than a noisy gong or a clanging bell. I may have the gift of inspired preaching; I may have all knowledge and understand all secrets; I may have all the faith needed to move mountains—but if I have no love, I am nothing. I may give away everything I have, and even give up my body to be burned—but if I have no love, this does me no good. Love is patient and kind; it is not jealous or conceited or proud; love is not ill mannered or selfish or irritable; love does not keep a record of wrongs; love is not happy with evil, but is happy with the truth. Love never gives up; and its faith, hope and patience never fail. Love is eternal. There are inspired messages, but they are temporary; there are gifts of speaking in strange tongues, but they will cease; there is knowledge but it will pass. For our gifts of knowledge and of inspired messages are only partial; but when what is perfect comes, then what is partial will disappear. When I was a child, my speech, feelings and thinking were all those of a child; now that I am a man, I have no more use for childish ways.

What we see now is like a dim image in a mirror; then we shall see face-to-face. What I know now is only partial; then it will be complete—as complete as God's knowledge of me. Meanwhile these three remain: faith, hope and love; and the greatest of these is love." (1 Corinthians 12: 1-13)

5

First Year of Marriage

As soon as we were settled in our little apartment, I began a search for a job. Each ad that I followed up on had a long line of applicants. The economy had not recovered from the war and many had been recently discharged from the service, so I took a job as a door-to-door salesman selling sterling silver tableware on commission. After several days of strong rejection, I decided that either I was a terrible salesman or the product was in very little demand.

Then I saw an ad for a chemist. I had taken all the chemistry courses I could in college because I liked it so much and it was good for pre-med. Could I convince a professional that I could do a chemist's job? Only way to find out was to apply and get an interview. I pushed my background as hard as I could without saying that I intended to return to medical school. The interviewer (the head chemist) asked if I was familiar with the iodate titration method for determining copper concentration. I stretched the truth by saying that I was, but hadn't done it for awhile and would need to refresh my knowledge. He said that was okay and hired me on the spot. I went straight to the library and learned the iodate titration method.

The job required a move to Ajo, a remote company town on the edge of a big open pit copper mine owned by Phelps Dodge. When I say remote, I mean *desolate*. It was far removed from any sign of civilization, on the edge of the Papago Indian reservation. I was concerned about the distance to Jeanne's doctors but they reassured me that I could give any medicine she needed including such things as IV aminophyllin.

There had been an air corps training facility in Ajo during the war and the base housing units, all temporary construction, were divided into small one room apartments and rented to workers. They were primitive. The water lines to the units were buried only a few inches beneath the desert sand, so during the hot days the water was hot enough to bathe in and wash dishes and clothes. We got cooler water from the hot water tank which was kept off allowing the water to cool somewhat.

The apartment was cooled with a window water cooler: a big perforated metal box lined with wood shavings through which water was dripped. A fan drew outside air through the damp shavings and cooled the air from about 120 degrees to about 100 degrees. Of course, it raised the humidity from near zero to "sticky" levels.

The biggest problem with the apartment was the presence of millions of cockroaches and many scorpions. No matter how much bug spray we used, they quickly migrated back from the adjacent apartment.

On my first day at work, the head chemist stood and looked over my shoulder as I did my first determination. He said that I did well and from that point on was on my own. I did about 100 determinations each day. Jeanne also worked as a nurse in the company hospital but we quickly learned that it was too much as her asthma continued.

I did my best to keep up with medicine by reading. One of my favorites was the weekly New England Journal of Medicine—the premier source of new clinical information. My favorite section was the weekly CPC (Clinical Pathological Conference) in which a case was presented exactly as it had been presented to the doctors. Then the laboratory and x-ray results were detailed. This was followed by an in-depth discussion by one or more of the professors leading to a diagnosis. Finally the results of autopsy (in case of death) or surgical findings were discussed by the pathologist. It provided an excellent learning tool and often left us with the impression that the pathologist is the only one who is always right!

As I would sit and read and study the case, Jeanne would look over my shoulder and frequently ask," I wonder if they did such-and-such a test?" Sure enough, in the next paragraph, the professor would ask the same question. She would do this, considering the aspects of the case almost in the same manner as the professor. The professor's conclusion was not always right, or would be included in a list or differential diagnosis. But Jeanne almost always focused right in on the correct answer. I knew she was an outstanding nurse (she scored the second highest grade in the state on her examinations and received a letter of commendation from the nursing board), but in this exercise she was competing with the best clinicians at the Massachusetts General Hospital. I was feeling badly that I could not do as well. After many weeks, she finally confessed that she had carefully unwrapped the journal, read it, and then rewrapped it so that it did not appear to have been opened. We had a real belly laugh over that.

During this time we purchased our first car. It was a 1936 Ford Model A Coupe that had sold eleven years earlier for about $400.00, and that is what we had to pay for it despite its age. Cars were in high demand after WWII.

It didn't take long for us to realize that the climate change made no measurable difference in Jeanne's asthma. She was experiencing just as much wheezing and shortness of breath and using as much medicine as she had in Chicago.

She was almost finished with her one year trial of Arizona's climate when the fall semester at Northwestern was scheduled to begin. I called the Dean and he agreed that I could start up where I left off, in the middle of my junior year. All the family and Jeanne's doctors agreed that we should come back to Chicago. Her parents were angels and let us move in with them as Caryl was off to college (Albion), and we could use her room. Cortisone, despite its many side effects, was being used more and more in treating refractory asthma so Jeanne was doing somewhat better. She was able to work in a hospital near home where as an RN she made only a dollar an hour (the going wage). How things have changed! I finished my junior year in December, right before our first anniversary.

6

Finishing School

I entered my senior year of medical school in January, 1949. This year the focus was on clinical medicine; a few lectures were offered but most of our time was devoted to patient contact. We performed histories and physicals and discussed them with clinical professors frequently in a one-on-one setting, or at least in very small groups. We followed patients in the hospital or the clinics and were quizzed daily by the attending physicians and residents.

We were living with Jeanne's parents, without whose help I cannot imagine how we would have managed. She was pregnant, due to deliver our first child in February, and worked almost to the end of the pregnancy. I rode the "El," short for elevated, from the end of the line which was near our home to Chicago Avenue, close to school. The medical and law schools were on what was called the Chicago Avenue campus. Undergraduate schools were in Evanston. The one hour ride each way gave me a little extra time to review notes before and after each day.

During this senior year, one of my clinical assignments was to the Chicago Maternity Center. This was a unique organization which provided prenatal care and delivery in the home. Charge for the service was minimal to none at all. Most of the patients were poor but occasionally a family, well able to afford the cost of private care and hospitalization, used the center because they preferred home delivery and were aware of the excellent results obtained at the center. High risk and complicated cases were scheduled to go to the hospital when labor began. Routine or uncomplicated cases were scheduled for delivery in their home.

Expectant mothers were advised to save a large pile of newspapers to prepare a semi-sterile bed for the delivery. (Apparently the ink on the newsprint acted as a bacterial suppressant.) They were also asked to boil a large pot of water as soon as they notified the Center that labor had begun. This was used to sterilize the instruments for delivery. If the patient was "a primip" (a first pregnancy), the team included an anesthesia resident (to administer a saddle block for pain control), an obstetric resident to perform the delivery including episiotomy and repair, and a junior medical student to prepare the table (yes, the kitchen table) and sterilize the instruments. If the patient was a "multip "(previous deliveries), a senior and junior medical student were dispatched and performed a normal vaginal delivery.

Between cases we had a cot to sleep on at the center. I doubt that it was changed with any frequency and I got bed bug bites one night. When my tour was over and I could go home for a day or two, Jeanne met me at the door and sent me to the basement to undress and put my clothes in the washing machine, then shower before coming upstairs. She didn't want to get bedbugs too.

During this senior year, our daughter Caryl was born in Wesley Hospital, the University Hospital of the time. The delivery was uncomplicated and Caryl was beautiful; so beautiful that she was selected for a photo session by Abbott Laboratories, to illustrate their advertisement for ABDEC, their new pediatric vitamin formula. She was given a check for $10 with the notation that it was a professional modeling fee. (That $10 was enough to cover the cost of the nursery for the five days; in those days nursery care was only an extra $2.00 per day). Actually we kept the check for years as a souvenir. I don't remember it ever being cashed.

The birth occurred at 8:20 AM which was the time of my psychiatry class. The next week, the professor asked why I had not been in class. When I told him that I was attending the birth of my first child, he informed me that that was not considered an excused absence. I wonder what the psychology of that decision was.

Jeanne remained at home for the next few weeks taking care of Caryl, and then returned to work while I attended classes. I had to take classes during the summer to at least partially catch up with my class, allowing me to graduate in December. One big advantage of December graduation was that I could choose my own Internship rather than go through the matching program. There was a single opening at Wesley Hospital (due to a last minute cancellation) and it was considered the best of all. I especially wanted it so that I could get on Gilbert Marquardt's service in internal medicine, as he was an outstanding teacher whose teaching style was the very best for me. It was a very busy service and very hard but between him and his two associates there was so much clinical experience that I felt I could diagnose and treat any disease known to man by the time I finished.

To be assigned to Marquardt's service, one had to also agree to be on Raymond McNeeley's surgery service. McNeeley had a reputation for being especially hard to work for particularly if you were an intern, the low man on the totem pole. He was an excellent and very busy surgeon, doing more cases in a week than most did in a month. He demanded that everything be done exactly according to his manual which was on each nurse's station. Any deviation meant a verbal thrashing in front of the staff and patient.

In the operating room never was a word spoken. All communication was done by sign language. It was an efficient, all business system. One day during a case I was the last assistant, holding a retractor, straining to see all that was going on. The circulating nurse came in and announced that an old patient of Dr. McNeeley's had come into the emergency room with severe abdominal pain. He turned to me and ordered me to "break scrub" and go see the patient. This patient had a long history of peptic (duodenal) ulcer and that morning had suddenly been seized with terrible abdominal pain. I quickly recognized that he had perforated and did the appropriate tests. The clincher of the diagnosis was the presence of free air under the diaphragm which showed up beautifully on his chest x-ray.

I talked to him and convinced him that he needed emergency surgery as soon as Dr. McNeeley finished his current case. He agreed and I notified the ER that this should be the next case. I gave him his pre op medicines which included morphine and collected all his lab work. I headed to the OR to inform Dr. McNeeley but he was already on his way to the ER. As he approached the patient, I recited the history and the physical and laboratory and x-ray data. He started to examine the patient's abdomen which already hurt less because of the medicine he had received.

Dr. McNeeley blew his stack and berated me violently in front of everyone, demanding whether or not I knew his rule that pain medicine was never to be administered until a diagnosis was established. I looked him right in the eye and announced that I had indeed established the diagnosis and the medication had been given as prep for his immediate surgery.

He looked me back in the eye and asked "did you get him to sign a permit before you gave him morphine"? When I told him that I had and that it was on the chart, he said that he had recommended surgery more than a year before but the patient would not give his permission.

We proceeded together to the OR. The operation went well (in silence as usual) and McNeeley showed all of us the perforation before he repaired it. As the final steps were being taken, sponge count, instrument check etc., he motioned for the needle and thread to close the incision. He then turned to me and asked "Reed, do you think you can close?" I said yes and he handed me the needle. I lined up the sides of the incision and took the first stitch in the center. He just turned away and left the OR. As soon as he was out of earshot, the chief resident remarked to me that he had never, ever let an intern do anything like this. This was the ultimate compliment from him. It was a great teaching service.

The remaining rotations on my internship were pediatrics, urology, psychiatry, thoracic surgery, neurology and emergency room. Time off during internship was rare. While theoretically we had every other night and every other weekend off, the night off did not begin before all work was done, which was rarely before 7-8 PM, and we were back on duty at 6 AM. The weekend was just over 24 hours: from about 2-3 PM on Saturday till about 6 PM on Sunday. A bunk bed adjacent to the ER was available to us when we were on duty.

We were still living with Jeanne's parents at this time and Jeanne was back at work at a nearby community hospital. Pay was only $1.00 per hour for an RN in the outlying hospitals but she could get to and from work quickly. She worked almost up to the time of our entry into the Air Force.

My class at Northwestern was the last one to receive a Bachelor of Medicine degree upon graduation, and we were not awarded our M.D. until we finished our internship. This gave the school control of where interns went for their training, and places without a good teaching staff were not approved. Wesley was the best.

In June 1950, right in the middle of my internship, the Korean War began. Congress passed a special draft law for physicians and it was clear that I would have to go back into the service at the end of my internship. The time I had spent in school during WWII did not count toward deferment, only the time I was working as a corpsman at Bainbridge Naval Hospital.

Before the draft started, I began application process with the Navy. When Dr. Marquardt (my chief at the time) learned of this he called me in and advised me to apply instead to the Air Force. The Army Air Corps was made an independent service in 1947. Marquardt had been the chief of Internal Medicine for the Air Corps at the end of WWII.

When the application became stalled and the draft was threatening, he called the Pentagon on my behalf and talked to the Surgeon General who was a friend of his. I overheard him asking about the health of "Hap" referring to General Hap Arnold who was the top ranking Air Force officer and whose serial number was 1. Mine was 23590.

That same day I received a telegram accepting me into the Air Force and quickly found an officer to swear me in. I received orders to active duty right at year's end but started my residency before deployment because the hospital had not yet recruited a replacement for me. I got in slightly over one month as a resident in Internal Medicine at Wesley before I had to report on February 12,

1951, to Chanute Air Force Base in Rantoul Illinois, where we began a new chapter in our lives.

7

The Air Force Years
February 12, 1951 to October 1, 1959

FIRST DUTY STATION

We had no idea what the Air Force had planned for us. The Korean War was in full swing but we hoped to have some time together before I was sent into the conflict. I was commissioned a first lieutenant, the bottom of the totem pole for medical officers, and expected very basic duties such as dispensary or routine "sick call." I was ordered to report to Chanute Air Force Base only 90 miles from Chicago. Instead, after being interviewed by the Commander of the hospital who was a very competent surgeon, I was assigned to dependent medicine (caring for the families of airmen) and ordered to establish an allergy service. This wasn't entirely unfounded; part of my internship had included three months on internal medicine with Gilbert Marquardt M.D. and one month with Dr. Leon Unger, professor of Allergy at Northwestern. In addition, I had completed my first month as a resident in internal medicine with Dr. Marquardt. The commander was impressed by the teachers I had worked under during my training and felt that I could handle significant responsibility. It was good duty for a very young doctor.

My orders specifically stated that I was authorized to ship our household goods to the base; what they didn't know was that all we owned was a refrigerator and a bed. The total shipping bill was $35.00, which doesn't sound like much but it was almost all our cash. I immediately went to the base finance office with my receipt to be reimbursed. Their reaction was that I should not have done it that way. I was supposed to place the request out for three bids. I was assured that I would get my money, but I had to fill out a detailed request and wait for it to be reviewed and approved. Well, 11 months and 22 days later I received approval for reimbursement of $34.10, as there was a $0.90 tax attached which the government was not responsible for. As crazy and inefficient as this sounds, I learned that it was not unusual.

We were assigned base housing at Chanute. This sounded great but our house was very small, one room which was partitioned into a bedroom and kitchen and with a coal furnace in one corner—and we were right in line with the main runway of the base. Planes flew very low over our house at all times of the night and day. We actually got so used to it that it was not a bother; at least until the day they landed a B36, which was the largest plane in the air force at that time. It had four J47 turbojet engines and six R-4360-53 piston engines. When it came over our place everything shook and it felt like it was only a few feet higher than our roof. It was designed to carry a nuclear bomb.

Despite the location and size, this was our first home and we were quite comfortable in it. We tilled a garden area in the back in the most fertile soil imaginable. Jeanne delighted in planting and caring for more fruits and vegetables than we could ever eat. We never had as rich a garden again. There was lots of room for Caryl to play outside, and many children her age in the neighborhood. At the end of my first month as a military officer, I received my pay, in cash. It was only a couple hundred dollars but seemed like a fortune. I came in the house and threw the money in the air. We counted it several times. We were truly happy with our home and my assignment. Jeanne and Caryl quickly adjusted to military life and when I was saluted, she would even return the salute.

After only a few weeks, I was ordered on TDY (temporary duty) to go to the first Air Force medical field service school at Gunter AFB, Montgomery, Alabama for two weeks of basic training in Air Force procedures, survival etc. Jeanne and Caryl stayed with the family in Chicago and both cried crocodile tears as I left. I felt like I was going to war. It was our first separation since our marriage.

A couple of months later, three of us who were classified as medical officer, general duty, were ordered to Brooks Army Hospital in San

Antonio, Texas, to take a one week course in Induction Station Procedures. We were assured that attendance at this course did not necessarily mean that we would be assigned to an induction station, but I was very suspicious that we would.

SECOND DUTY STATION

Sure enough, a few weeks after the San Antonio course I was ordered to the Enlistment and Induction Station in Toledo, Ohio. This meant that I was responsible for the physical examination of volunteers and inductees—about the worst job a young doctor can get, especially when he is convinced that he is a great diagnostician and should be taking care of sick patients. We rented a small apartment and Jeanne adjusted instantly and made many friends. Soon, we felt at home. Ann was born during this assignment, and as the delivery date drew near, Jeanne went to stay with her parents in La Grange, a suburb of Chicago. We both wanted the birth to take place in Wesley Hospital where we had trained, and to have the same obstetrician we had for Caryl's delivery.

I was at work when Jeanne called to tell me that her waters had broken about two hours earlier. I asked her if she remembered what the average time to delivery was for a "multip" after waters breaking. She remembered that it was about two hours. I advised her to get on the way to the hospital immediately and asked the Captain of our station for emergency leave to go to Chicago for the birth. We had finished the day's physicals and only paper work remained to be done, which I felt

The Air Force Years

the staff could complete. He said no, I couldn't leave till after the station closed for the day, but he did give me two days off. I rushed to the hospital and arrived a couple of hours after Ann's birth. The nurses brought her out for me to see. She was beautiful and I was so proud. Jeanne was fine and had a normal delivery with no flare up of her asthma. After a few days in La Grange, she was able to return to Toledo, now with two little ones to keep her busier than ever. Despite her asthma, which was continuous, she managed without complaint.

The job at the Enlistment and Induction station was a real bore with way too much paper work and I longed to get back to real medicine. Soon, another opportunity presented itself. It was a chance to go back to my residency in return for a period of obligated service. This sounded reasonable so I applied, fully expecting to go back to Wesley Hospital.

THIRD DUTY STATION

Surprise! Instead, I was accepted and ordered to report to the Veterans Hospital in Indianapolis. I decided to drive to Indianapolis and see what was in store for us before trying to get out of the deal because I thought there was no place that could compare with Wesley as a place to train in internal medicine. When we arrived in town, I asked directions to the hospital and was sent to the old hospital on Fort Benjamin Harrison. It seemed more like a medical warehouse than a training hospital. I met the director and he told me that I was at the wrong place. A new hospital had just opened in the medical center adjacent to the medical school. When I got there, I talked to the residents and found that, in their opinion, I could not have come to a better place because of a certain teacher, Dr. Patrick Genovese. Dr. Genovese was the assistant chief of medicine and a gifted and dedicated teacher. His teaching technique was exactly what I had admired in Dr. Marquardt. I don't believe he ever answered a question of mine without responding with a question of his own that would start me thinking and searching the literature for the answer. He taught me so much that I stayed at Veterans for the full three years and felt very well trained, indeed.

Jeanne was my strength during this time and made many friends, getting us involved in social and church activities. Her asthma remained moderate but steroids would always bail her out when the going got rough. She never complained, even when she struggled for breath. Like most residencies, I was frequently on duty all night and on many weekends. Time at home was limited and so much of the work of raising our family fell on Jeanne.

During this period of residency, Jeanne became pregnant and Joel III was born on September 28, 1953. After the delivery, the doctor left the delivery room and went on his rounds without talking to me. The wait seemed excessively long and I began to panic that something terrible was going on. I finally got up and went to the door and asked about Jeanne and her labor. The nurse asked if the doctor had not talked to me. When I answered no, I was still waiting, they put in a page for him and he came down and told me he had just forgotten to look for me in the waiting room. Talk about terrible bedside manner! Jeanne, as usual, did well and her asthma had not flared up during the delivery. Now she had three children to care for, a five year old, a two year old and a newborn, but she handled it all better than most with only one. What a wonderful mother she was. She always had time for each one, so much so, that each felt that they were like an only child. To this day, each of our children refers to himself or herself as 'Your favorite." The girls would start any phone conversation with "This is your favorite daughter," and with her quick wit, Jeanne would always reply, "Oh hello _____," and then use the name of one of the others.

Poliomyelitis was still rampant during these years. Parents with children feared the summer season. The only preventive measure we knew was to avoid crowds, swimming pools or playgrounds. Fortunately, school was not in session in the summer so that exposure at least was avoided. Polio was so prevalent that there were special hospitals with rehabilitation facilities. An example was TIRR (Texas Institute for Rehabilitation and Research) in Houston, where row upon row of Drinker Respirators (the large tank that supported breathing) functioned for those whose respiration was compromised by the paralysis. One summer during my residency, Jeanne's sister and brother-in law offered to come down to Indianapolis for a week-end and care for the children so that we could go to the Indiana State Park for a break.

George was working on his PhD at Purdue which was only a few miles away. Jeanne was really fatigued as her chronic asthma was more active. The getaway was delightful. We left on a Friday evening, and on Saturday, we relaxed, hiked, swam, and napped—but the high point was the time we were able to spend conversing without the thousands of interruptions that children make as they compete for attention. It was like a honeymoon.

Early Sunday morning we were awakened by a call from George that Ann had complained of a headache and had a low grade fever the night before, and when she awoke she could not stand. Of course, I panicked as these are the classical symptoms of polio. We literally threw our things in the car and headed home, driving well beyond the speed limit. I developed a painful tightness in my chest and told Jeanne that, if a patient presented to me with the same symptom, I would suspect a heart attack. I diagnosed myself as having cardio spasm due to stress. As soon as we arrived home I checked Ann and found a stiff neck and marked weakness in her legs. I called our pediatrician who met us at the hospital. After his examination he announced that she had polio and that we should take her home and observe her, especially her breathing. I asked why he did not do a spinal tap. He responded that the diagnosis was so certain that it would not add anything and only cause more discomfort. I also asked why he was not admitting her to the hospital. He replied that since Jeanne was a registered nurse and I was a physician, he was sure that we would watch her more closely than she would have been watched in the hospital. How right he was. We watched every breath.

It was usual for me to panic whenever there was an illness or injury to anyone in the family. I am sure that Jeanne felt as much tension as I, but she always remained calm using her energy to reach a solution. Ann improved slowly over the next few days and we were grateful for the way the pediatrician had handled the problem. She had no residual effects and her recovery was complete.

The residency training went well and thankfully the children had no more serious illnesses. Caryl did experience frequent sore throats and had very large tonsils. Radiation therapy to shrink the tonsils was recommended by our pediatrician and our ENT man, as it was a popular approach at that time. It was not successful however, and eventually Caryl had to have the tonsils surgically excised because of their very large size. The radiation approach was eventually abandoned by the profession because of increased risk of thyroid cancer. Caryl has been checked regularly ever since. Ann had crossed eyes and had to wear special glasses to correct them. She hated those glasses.

NEXT DUTY STATION

My residency in Internal Medicine was in its final weeks when I received orders from the Air Force that my next duty station would be the 6208th USAF Hospital in the Philippines. My first thoughts were of jungles, mosquitoes, and primitive medical facilities. A colleague received orders the same day to Burtonwood Air Force base in England. He received many compliments on his fine assignment. I received mostly good wishes. It seemed a job well below my qualifications. Later that year, we exchanged letters and his grand duty was a dispensary where he treated mostly colds and minor ailments, and his housing was a Quonset hut which was always cold.

The 6208th turned out to be a referral center for most of Southeast Asia with a staff which included most specialties and a reasonably well equipped hospital. I was the chief of medicine with several internists and the psychiatry service under my responsibility. From a professional aspect, it was a great place to be. Bob Hope referred to it in one of his broadcasts as the only country club in the world with its own Air Force.

I immediately started to process for the move. When I asked what arrangements were necessary to move my wife and three children, I was given the very bad news that I couldn't even apply for their transfer until I was on duty in the Philippines and that there was a long waiting list. They didn't know how long it would be but that I could find out when I arrived.

Deep depression quickly set in. Jeanne and I had not been apart more than a week since our marriage began. The children were 6, 3, and 1½ years old. I knew this would be a painful period but I vowed to pull every string I could to speed the process. We used all the leave I had to make a leisurely trip to San Francisco, my departure point. We went to the Grand Canyon for a few days and Jeanne and I rode the mules to the bottom, spent the night in the lodge there, and rode the mules back up. What a gutsy gal she was. We also stopped in Las Vegas just long enough to learn that you don't ever win for long.

The time for my departure came too soon. My "bird" was a military super Constellation, a big and powerful propeller aircraft. With several refuelings, we would reach Clark AFB after nearly thirty hours.

The first bad omen of our arrival was the pilot's announcement that we had a potential emergency: the plane's nose wheel had failed to lock in position. He made a long low approach to the runway, and we could see the fire trucks and ambulances racing alongside us as we landed. Then the plane settled down ever so gently and held. No crash, and only one casualty: a crewman hung down from a small hatch in the cabin and inserted a pin manually to prevent collapse of the nose wheel. In doing so, he lost his grip and fell about twelve feet to the tarmac dislocating his shoulder.

We arrived on a Sunday, so there was nothing I could do but check into the bachelor officer's quarters, a Quonset hut, and wait for the next morning.

My first stop on Monday was to the housing office to get some idea of the wait to send for my family. To my amazement, the housing officer told me that houses were immediately available. I could apply that very day but could not move in until my family was aboard ship and on their way to the Philippines. I asked why they couldn't have told me that when I first got my orders and we could have travelled together. He responded that this was the way the Air Force did it. The worst news was that it would take about three months to complete the paper work and be issued orders for them to come. The biggest delay would be in getting passports since this was the beginning of tourist season. Passports had to be in hand before the processing could begin.

I raced back to the BOQ and tried to place a phone call to Jeanne, but learned that for such a call I needed to make an appointment at least 24 hours in advance. I set up the call for the earliest time I could. It was radio telephone by short wave. After each statement we made it was necessary to say "over." Then the operator would switch so that the other person could respond. Between static and garbled phrases, we spent most of the time saying "what did you say?" That call cost $25.00, a big chunk of my pay then.

Frustrated by the lack of clear communication, I immediately wrote Jeanne a letter and raced to the base post office. One of her first letters confirmed the long delay in getting passports at that season. A call to his congressman by her father quickly solved that! Passports would be issued in a few days, he said. But there was no speeding the "shot" schedule or the slow processing of the paper work.

Finally, the orders came for Jeanne and the children to proceed to San Francisco. Jeanne thought it strange that that they were addressed to Mrs. Lt. Richard Reed, but she assumed it was the usual SNAFU and she would get it straight in San Francisco. No amount of protesting would get them to change the papers on board, and she was assigned to a cabin as Mrs. Lt. Richard Reed.

The Air Force Years

(As Mrs. Capt. Joel Reed she would have gotten a larger cabin. Rank has its privileges). She called me just before sailing to confirm that she was aboard.

The ship was the MSTS Barrett, a converted President's Liner, a true cruise ship with much of the space changed to bunks for the enlisted troops. It took 19 to 20 days for the crossing. The Air Force routinely approved leave for officers to return to San Francisco to accompany their families when there were small children. However, I had used up all my leave for our trip to the coast before I embarked. There was a possibility that I could fly to Guam and accompany them the last 4-5 days. We decided that would be better than to borrow the entire next year's leave. In retrospect, that was a bad decision, and my fault. I wish now that I had borrowed the leave and been able to help Jeanne care for the three children. It was a daunting task keeping up with three little ones aboard ship, but, as usual, she made the difficult look easy.

My depression was lifting rapidly, replaced by excitement and exhilaration at the prospect of seeing Jeanne and the children. I went to the housing office to claim the keys to our house so that I could get it ready for their arrival. Officers' housing at Clark was the best I had seen in the Air Force: tropical style with a screened porch all around to give maximum ventilation as there was no air conditioning. There was a large living/dining area, three bedrooms, a kitchen and maid's quarters adjacent to the kitchen. Everyone had live-in help. It would be a tropical paradise for us.

As the housing officer pored over his papers his frown became more and more apparent. Finally he looked up and announced to me that "your wife is not on the Barrett. It is Lt. Richard Reed's wife. He is ahead of you on the waiting list." I assured him of my telephone call the preceding day that it was indeed my wife and that she had been unable to correct the name on the orders. He was adamant that his paper work could not be incorrect and that she was the Lieutenant's wife. I tried to get him to call Lt. Reed to confirm that his wife was still in the US awaiting orders. He outranked me and would not back down. Finally I asked him," Does she have to sleep with him when she gets here because your papers say she is his wife?" That got results. He gave me the key.

(In Jeanne's words) It was spring of 1955, Joel had finished his Air Force Residency at the University of Indiana, Indianapolis, and it was time to move on. We had asked for an assignment in Hawaii—didn't everyone? But we, like so many others, were denied our first choice and also our second. The Air Force had bigger and better plans for us: The Philippines and illustrious Clark AFB! We didn't know what to expect.

In the years since our marriage in 1947, we'd had three children—2 girls and a boy, a six year old, a three year old and a 20 month old—quite a group to transport half way around the world. Joel left for overseas in May, while the children and I stayed in Chicago with my parents and grandparents until it came our time to make the big move. Happily that time came sooner than expected. Joel had found that he could get housing almost immediately. He called me by radio phone to let me know—the kind of call where you speak and then say "over" so the caller can respond to the callee. We spent most of the time saying to each other, "What did you say?" All of this cost $25 for three minutes, and remember, these are 1955 dollars!

Our top priority now was to get passports, shots and paper work completed. All was set for a flight to San Francisco on July 18, 1955, with embarkation on July 25 on the USNS Barrett.

Previous to this the children were moderately ill from their shots and the weather in Chicago was extremely hot. The baby hadn't had on much more than a diaper in the past two weeks. When it came time to dress him for the flight he didn't know how to act and kept rolling on the floor trying to get his clothes off.

The trip to San Francisco took eight long hours. By the time we arrived I looked like a wreck—a torn dress and three very tired babies. Our next stop was the port of embarkation where we were assigned a room while we spent the next few days finalizing details. The weather was in the 50's and all children were coming down with colds. No one told me that we would have to go through "winter" to get to our island paradise.

When I arrived at the staging area I was told that that my husband was Lt. Richard Reed. "No, no, I'm Capt. Joel Reed's wife." My papers proved my identity, they changed the name and I was at ease. Meanwhile, in the Philippines, another part of the story was being played out. Joel had gone to the housing office to be assigned a house. They told him that Mrs. Richard Reed was on the ship, not me. Joel was not to be denied, saying he had talked to me in San Francisco and that I was, indeed, on the ship. Joel's final question was, "Does she have to sleep with him before we can have a house?" That did it and they assigned Joel a house.

The children and I were on our way again within a few days. Bands were playing as we boarded our ship for the Philippines. Most of us were teary eyed; happy we were on our way and also wondering what lay ahead for us. We watched the San Francisco skyline fade as we sailed under the Golden Gate Bridge to a whole new adventure.

HOW I FOOLED THE NAVY

As the day approached when the ship would reach Guam, I borrowed enough leave and got it approved. I also filled out the routine request to board the Barrett, automatic for Captains and higher ranking officers. I arranged for a flight to Agana, Guam, on a military plane for that Sunday morning. About an hour before the scheduled takeoff, I received a telephone call from the base communications officer. He said that he had just received a TWX (telegram) from the port transportation officer in Guam that I had been denied permission to board the Barrett. (This was the old bugaboo about her being the Lieutenant's wife and the fact that she had been assigned the smaller quarters.) My spirits were too high to let any obstacle get in my way.

I asked him "Can you do a big favor for me?"

He replied, "I'll do anything I can."

"Can you say that you were unable to find me? After all it is Sunday morning and less than an hour till I board the plane."

He said "no problem, Good luck."

It was Sunday and only a few Navy personnel were on duty at Agana, Guam, that day. I went straight to the port transportation office and entered a small room. A very young petty officer was behind the desk. I announced that I was Captain Reed and was there to pick up my orders to board the ship which was just pulling into the harbor. He looked down, shuffled some papers around and asked, "Didn't you receive our TWX?" You were denied permission to board." I said, "No, there must be a mix-up. The port transportation officer is a friend of mine and he assured me it was okay." (Weeks before.) I told him to type up the orders and I would take them to be properly signed. He looked at me as if he knew that I was pulling a fast one on him but he was intimidated enough to turn to the typewriter and type out the official orders (of course unsigned).

I went to the docks where the ship was now berthed and could see Jeanne and the children on the upper deck. We waved frantically at each other. After what seemed to be an eternity, boarding began. I got in the middle of the pack, climbed the gangway, saluted the flag and the officer of the deck and handed him my unsigned orders hoping that, in the rush, he would not notice. An angel must have smiled on me at that moment for he plunked my papers on the stack and welcomed me aboard.

What a happy reunion! We found each other and hugged and kissed as the ship slowly pulled away from the dock and out of the harbor. Big ships start very slowly; they seem to not be moving at all. A half hour later we were still what looked to be only a stone's throw from the beaches when I heard on the loud speaker, "Captain Reed! Report to the Captain's office." My face fell. They must have found my unsigned orders. Would they put me in a dingy and row me to the shore, I wondered, or put me in the brig? I stalled as long as I dared hoping we would be too far at sea to put me overboard.

As I entered the Captain's office, a young Navy medical officer got up and addressed me.

"I have several very sick patients in sick bay. Would you please consult with me on them" he asked?

My spirits rebounded. I said "I will be very happy to see them and follow them with you for the rest of the trip."

The next four days were indeed paradise. The Navy never found out I was sailing with unsigned orders, or if they did, they never said so.

CLARK AIR FORCE BASE

Once the family arrived in the Philippines, we settled in quickly at Clark Air Force Base. There were good schools for Caryl and Ann and lots of playmates for Joel who was only 22 months old. He had a pet duck, a present from our full time, live in maid, and he loved to play outside. We also had a gardener and a part time laundress who took care of the washing and ironing. Jeanne finally had help to reduce the stress on her asthma, but she did not slow down, she just focused her energy elsewhere, teaching nursing at the hospital and taking golfing lessons so that we could play together.

My duty hours were the lightest I had had after several years of training where I worked almost every other night and weekend. I was promoted to Major and as a result I no longer had to take emergency room (MOD) duty, though I was always subject to call for consultations.

Access to medical care at Clark still followed the old system of sick call at 8 AM, to be seen by any one of the junior officers regardless of specialty with referral to the hospital if tests or x-rays and /or consultation were needed. The same process was repeated at 1PM. It was a very inefficient method of health care delivery.

I wanted to improve the system and proposed to the Hospital Commander that we use one of the vacant wings of the hospital as an outpatient clinic where patients could be seen by the appropriate specialist by appointment, thus bypassing sick call. In this way the patient would lose less time from work and the physician could focus directly on the problem. He agreed and we proceeded with the plan. It worked beautifully with a high degree of satisfaction on the part of both patient and doctor. Patients were losing less time at work and evaluations could be made as an outpatient, saving the expense to the Air Force of hospitalization.

Then one day the commander came to me and said, "Joel, you must close the clinic now!" I was astounded and asked why.

He responded "You must understand that our budget is based upon the percent of hospital bed occupancy," not on how much satisfaction there was with time saved or efficient care. I asked him to let me fly to Washington and show them how much time and money we were saving the Air Force, but he was adamant saying, "Don't rock the boat." I think he feared that if the higher-ups did not approve our process it would be hard on him and adversely affect his chances for promotion.

We used the time at Clark to make many friends, and to see a lot of Luzon, with our favorite place being Baguio City in the mountains. Little Joel had very blond hair and the natives (Igorots, former headhunters) would come up and touch his head in wonder.

I am not sure if there was a rule that we could not travel together outside of the PI but we decided early on that we would not. Jeanne was referred one time to an ENT Surgeon in Tokyo for consultation so she got a taste of Japan and Taiwan, and travelled to Hong Kong a couple of times with one of the other wives on shopping trips. Whenever someone went to Hong Kong they had a list of things to get for others as well as for themselves. I got to Japan twice with one of the trips to take my written part of the Internal Medicine Board exams. While on that trip, I was walking along with one of the other officers when a Japanese man came up from behind us and said," I got gulls (girls)." We told him we were not interested but he persisted," I got college gulls, they are cleaner." We again shooed him away and felt that we could more quickly discourage him by saying, "We aren't interested, we are homosexual." Even that did not stop him. He simply changed his pitch, saying "Oh, I got velly (very) fine homo show." Having no success he finally left us alone.

I expected the worst on the exam, but it seemed unusually easy for me because of my excellent training. When I returned, Jeanne fully expected me to complain how hard it had been and my appearance suggested that was true. But the only really hard part was the flight back. We had flown either too close to or actually into a thunderstorm and I got seriously airsick. I had thought I was immune as this had never happened before. It reminded me of the joke that "I was so sick, I was afraid I might die. Then as it got even worse, I was afraid that I might not." Jeanne said that I was white as a sheet when I got off the plane.

During our tour there, I had my first serious illness. Joel III caught the mumps and was very uncomfortable, one time, pointing to his cheeks, he cried "band aids, band aids" since, in his mind, that was the usual treatment for pains and injuries. He couldn't sleep well so came to bed with us, resting his head upon my shoulder. I didn't fear catching the mumps because I had been told that I had them as a child though I had no memory of that illness. That must not have been true, however, since as Joel III recovered, I came down with them. In fact, I came down hard with very high and persistent fever, abdominal pain and orchitis. My temperature was not controllable at home so I was admitted to the hospital where for 4 days my temp kept going back to 104 degrees and came down only with ice and alcohol rubs.

I was a little delirious at times, suggesting that I also had encephalitis and my abdominal pain suggested pancreatitis, all known complications of mumps. Though I was extremely uncomfortable, I certainly never felt critical, but my physician pulled Jeanne aside and said," we are doing everything possible." She interpreted that as a warning that I might die, but finally, I began to improve. I reached for my cigarettes which I had not had for several days. As I lit the first one, I thought that this was a perfect time to quit. I have never touched another one. After being fed intravenously for four days I still did not have an appetite. Jeanne was very solicitous offering to make anything I would like but nothing sounded tempting. Finally I thought of the broth they served at the Officer's Club. Jeanne went there and asked for some. The waiter returned with a can of Campbell's consommé. We had a good laugh over that. It still tasted good.

About two weeks after my recovery, I developed phlebitis (clots) in my right leg. It responded quickly to dicoumerol (blood thinner) and all seemed to return to normal until 32 years later; but more about that in another chapter.

Jeanne's asthma remained controllable during our whole time in the Philippines, though it required several rounds of steroids.

We loved the Philippino people and became close to our maid, Lucilia Deleon, and our yard boy, Reynaldo David. On one occasion we were invited by Lucy to dinner at her home, a nipa house which is the typical grass hut on stilts. I was on duty and could not go but Jeanne went with the children. The main course was a pig roasted outdoors on an open fire. All enjoyed it very much and I felt guilty that I didn't find someone to take my duty that day. Reynaldo invited us to "Fiesta" on Good Friday. That was the day when there was a parade and the "flagelantes," those who carry a cross and are whipped, finally being tied to the cross. They wear masks so that they will not be recognized, as the Catholic Church did not approve of the practice. We assumed that Reynaldo's invitation was to view the parade with him. We asked Lucy what time we should go because that had not been specified in the invitation. She told us that he was expecting us all for dinner before the parade.

We arrived and climbed the ladder into his nipa house, entering the living area. It was not really divided into rooms, just screened into sitting, cooking and sleeping areas. Reynaldo's father spoke little English but we conversed with him as well as we could. We were served a banana and a Coke while we waited for dinner. He noted our discomfort over what to do with the banana peels once we finished our snack. He took them from us and tossed them out of the window; a moment later we heard the pigs snorting as they consumed the unexpected treat.

The dinner was water buffalo, quite tasty but a little tough, and a vegetable mix which looked more like chop suey, rice and baluts (14-day duck embryos). Baluts are a delicacy in Asia but I could never bring myself to try them. Jeanne asked what that they were and was told chicken livers. She and the children all ate them but I hid mine under a lettuce leaf and did not try it. I had put my knife to it and could feel the little soft bones. Dessert was flan which is popular in many countries of Spanish influence.

After dinner we all went to the parade and were a bit taken aback but not horrified by the flagelantes, probably because we had been forewarned. When we got back home on base, the children went out to play. Jeanne and I were sitting quietly on the sofa looking at each other but not talking. Finally Jeanne asked me what I was thinking. My response was "I am just waiting to see who will get sick first". My concern was because I knew the meat and groceries were purchased at the market in Angeles, which was off limits to air force personnel because it was so unsanitary by American standards. The good news was that none of us had any ill effects at all!

As our tour was drawing to a close, we had several decisions to make. Since we were overseas, we had the opportunity to select our next base if it also was overseas. We seriously considered asking for Germany as the Air Force had some excellent hospitals there. But we had been away from family for two years and Jeanne's grandparents were getting quite old. We feared they might not last through another two to three year deployment.

So we decided to return to the states and take whatever assignment the Air Force offered.

The usual transportation for Air Force families (and we had three children) was by ship. That meant a three week ocean voyage. It would be a great time to be together and relax, and I could study for the oral, practical, and clinical parts of my specialty board examinations. The port transportation officer in Manila was a patient of mine and, since there were no Generals aboard our ship, he arranged for the biggest and finest suite for us. The day before departure we packed our thirteen suitcases (remember this was a three week cruise for five people) and went to bed. We were fearful of one thing. There was an epidemic of measles on the base (this was before measles vaccine) and we hoped the children would not come down with it. During the night, Caryl was coughing, often an early sign of measles. I lay there praying that she would not break out before we were aboard ship. No such luck. In the morning, she was florid with the typical measles rash.

I called the ships medical officer and pleaded with him to let us board, telling him that he was going to have an outbreak anyhow since all the children to board had surely been exposed in school. He knew that, but needed to follow regulations which prohibited him from boarding an active case.

We settled in for the next two weeks while Caryl recovered and prepared instead for a flight home by military aircraft. Our plane was a twin engine Convair, a slow propeller-driven craft. The route was Clark AFB—Agana, Guam—Kwajalein

Atoll—Johnson Is.—Honolulu, Hawaii—San Francisco, California—then commercial air to Chicago (for my board exam) and finally to San Antonio, Texas (Lackland Air Force Base).

When we landed at Agana, Guam, for refueling, we waited in the terminal which was a large Quonset hut. As I strolled around to pass the time, I looked up and saw Dr. Gilbert Marquardt my chief and mentor during my internship and the start of my residency in internal medicine at Wesley. He had also been the family internist for Jeanne and her family and was the one who had advised me to join the Air Force rather than the Navy. We, almost simultaneously asked each other "What are you doing here?" I explained that we were returning from our tour of duty in the Philippines and he said that he was on an official inspection tour of the Far East for the Surgeon General. Isn't it a small world? We had a fine reunion discussing all that had gone on since we were last together. He was especially interested in the progress of Jeanne's asthma.

Our flight took about 35 hours in the air to reach the U.S. With three children, we worried that it would be very hard for them. But they took the trip well, probably better than we did, and best of all, we arrived home sooner than if we had been on the ship.

During our stay in Chicago before reporting to Lackland, I was able to finish my board exams. These sections included identification of microscopic slides, photographs and actual specimens. Finally I was assigned two patients to examine and was then questioned afterward by two examiners who were prepared with tough questions. As I walked in to meet one of the examiners, he handed me a slide and pointed to the microscope. I gulped, fearful that it would be something I wouldn't recognize. After all, microscopic pathology is not a strong part of Internal Medicine training. Internists are called diagnosticians. Well. I focused on the slide and breathed a sigh of relief. I recognized it immediately as sarcoidosis and reeled off a description which was almost word for word from the textbooks. He complimented me on my description and conclusion. As I sat down, he asked "did you see any asteroid bodies?" I started back toward the microscope to take another look. Before I took my second step, I turned to him and said "There is no use looking, I don't even know what an asteroid body is." He laughed and told me that it had just been described in a recent article which I had not had a chance to read. I think I got more credit for my honesty than I did for my accurate diagnosis.

THE FIFTH DUTY STATION

We had a nice visit with the family before we headed out for San Antonio and Lackland Air Force Base. Jeanne was pregnant with Mary and due to deliver in a couple weeks. No base housing was available and the only housing we could afford was on the opposite side of town. We worried about the distance and whether or not we would make it to the hospital after labor began. So with the first contraction, we rushed to the base hospital. She was put to bed and observed with only minor contractions for nearly 24 hours. The doctor came in and said that it had been "false labor" and that he was going to send her home. At that very moment, her contractions really hit hard and Jeanne said "No you won't."

She delivered about 20 minutes later without even enough time to get a pudendal block for pain control which had been planned. Mary was beautiful and thankfully, Jeanne's asthma did not flare up and we now had four little ones with two in school.

At Lackland I was assigned to the pulmonary service under Colonel Stonehill, who was a great teacher and world expert on pulmonary function. It was a fine place to be and a very busy service. I became intensely interested in pulmonary disease and pulmonary function mostly because of Jeanne but also because of the excellent mentoring of Col. Stonehill. He was very strict and demanded excellence and was affectionately called "old iron pants."

My passion for pulmonary diseases would persist for the rest of my medical practice. I was trained in bronchoscopy the old fashioned way with the rigid scope. I was able to do several hundred while at Lackland Air Force base and participated in pulmonary function research and in altitude research, even publishing a couple of articles with Col. Stonehill. Our clinical research on pneumonia was never published but we learned a great deal from the over 1500 cases of pneumonia we treated during the 1957 Asian flu epidemic. This was also the time of the early application of mechanical ventilation with the Byrd respirator.

I also had the opportunity to become a flight surgeon and underwent special training including ejection seat, altitude chamber, and explosive decompression. When I was finally qualified, Jeanne asked me to check with my life insurance to be sure that my policy included coverage for flight in single engine jets. It did not, and to purchase a rider would cost double the usual premium. That told us a lot about the risk; as a result I opted to get most of my flying hours in propeller aircraft.

Jeanne's asthma was fairly stable thanks to lots of steroids. She hated them because of the obvious and the hidden side effects. Even small doses caused sleeplessness and we worried about the loss of bone mass and impaired infection resistance. We tried to taper the dose to very small amounts, even every other day dosage, but as soon as the doses got very small or if we tried to discontinue them, she would have an exacerbation and it would take a few days to settle things down again. Fortunately, inhalation steroids became available and the systemic dosage was markedly reduced.

Finally, government housing became available to us and we moved on base. The apartments were small, but the convenience of being on base was worth the crowding. We were close to the schools, the PX, and the hospital, none over 5 minutes away. I had much more time with the family. This was about as good as could be in the Air Force. My pay was not bad as I was qualified for specialty pay (certified by the Board of Internal Medicine), longevity pay (generously including my Navy time), and flight pay as a flight surgeon. I was required to get a minimum of 100 hours flight time each year and no less than ten hours in any month. Jeanne was a "white knuckles" flyer's wife, worrying each time I was off flying. She had no such trouble when we were together on a flight. I did have three scary situations including an unlocked nose wheel landing (it did not collapse), a ground loop accident (no injuries), and a loss of one engine on takeoff in a C45. Fortunately the pilot was able to set down a few feet before the crash barrier.

We were really quite content and felt that the Air Force would be our career when a friend in the Pentagon called me to tell me what he felt was good news: I was to be transferred to Orlando AFB as chief of professional services. To him and the brass, this was considered a promotion and would be followed shortly by a real promotion to Lt. Col. To me it meant more paper work and less patient care. The latter was my real love. He agreed to get it squashed and I again felt comfortable. In only a few weeks he called again to tell me I was being sent to Scott AFB also as chief of professional services and this one could not be stopped except by my resignation before the orders arrived.

That day I went home for lunch and a long discussion with Jeanne about the prospects of suddenly resigning with no plans on where we might go to start a practice. We did not make such decisions without agreement on both our parts, but Jeanne was always so supportive of me that I was never sure if a decision really reflected her own desire or whether she read my mind and supported me. She got the typewriter out and we wrote a letter of resignation which I took to Col. Stonehill and to the hospital commander and both were astounded as all felt (me included) that I was in the Air Force for the long haul. As close as our professional relationship had been, it cooled dramatically after I submitted the letter.

A job search ensued immediately. Chicago was first on our list because of Jeanne's family and it was where we both had trained. Also, a cardiologist friend had just gotten out of service and was planning on opening an office in Oak Park or La Grange. We were very compatible and close friends, so it seemed to be a good decision. We even looked at office space and we were discussing the possibility of partnership. While still pondering this decision, a pulmonologist in Dallas offered me the chance to join him. This offer was attractive but I felt that our personalities would conflict: he was much too business oriented. Then I was offered a chance to join the Baylor Faculty but the pulmonary opening was at the TB hospital and I wanted a broader patient base.

Finally, a friend advised me to talk to one of the founders of a new private internal medicine group in Houston called the Diagnostic Clinic of Houston. It was right across the street from Baylor University Medical School and less than a block away from Methodist, Hermann, and St. Luke's hospitals. Most subspecialties were already represented but they were looking for a pulmonologist. Diagnostic offered all the things I wanted including the opportunity to teach the residents at Hermann Hospital both rounding on their hospitalized patients and supervising them in the clinics. Hermann was both a private and charity hospital. For the next 30 years and 3 months Diagnostic Clinic was to be my base. I started work as a civilian in private practice on October 1, 1959.

8

Finally, Private Practice

During our final weeks in the Air Force, we purchased a home in Southwest Houston in a development called Westbury, seven miles from the clinic where I was to work. The house was still under construction at the time we made the deal and Jeanne was able to pick all the finishing touches such as the cabinets, fixtures, wall paper, paint colors, etc. It had the largest lot in the subdivision because the street it faced and the street to the back diverged. The oddly shaped lot had three neighbors to one side, three to the back and one on the other side. It was ideal for our growing family of four children varying in age from 2 to 10 years.

This was the first house we had ever owned. I had accumulated over two months of leave time so with the lump sum payment that I received from the Air Force, we were able to make the down payment. Money was short, however, because I had to take a pay cut to accept the clinic job. My Air Force pay was inflated because of specialty pay (board certified internist), flight pay (flight surgeon), and longevity pay (included my Navy time). Cash flow was slow—so slow that it took over two years before we could furnish the living and dining rooms.

We were busy from day one (October 1, 1959); I with getting a practice started; Jeanne with getting a new house organized, getting three children to and from school while caring for the fourth at home, getting involved in the community and church affairs, and handling the shopping, finances and a thousand more things. Her job must have been a hundred times bigger and busier than mine but at the time I never realized how much she accomplished because she always made it look easy and never complained.

Added to this was our fifth pregnancy. John was born on August 9th, 1960. With his arrival, we needed help. While still in the Air Force in San Antonio, we enjoyed part time housekeeping help from a wonderful lady, Estella Teneyucca, whom we loved as did all the children. She was like a member of the family. We called her to see if she could come to Houston and help for a few weeks. She did, and except for vacations, she remained with us as part of the family until her untimely death from a massive stroke in 1978. We could never again hire fulltime help because we had all become so attached to her.

Even with Stella's help, I cannot imagine how Jeanne made her job seem so easy. When I hear complaints from parents of one or two or three children about how busy they are, I only wonder more about how Jeanne handled it all with never a negative word. She was an angel.

Tragedy came in 1963 when Jeanne miscarried a sixth pregnancy and hemorrhaged enough to require a transfusion. This was in the days before blood was tested for hepatitis, which we think may have been the source of the hepatitis C that caused Jeanne's death 45 years later. Another suspected cause was gamma globulin injections Jeanne received in the early 1970's. A research article reported that immune globulin could modify asthma. It didn't help Jeanne and also may have been the source of the hepatitis C. The theory that it was useful for treating asthma was later debunked.

My practice was very successful and our income was sufficient to send all five of the children to private schools and to Texas Christian University for college. When Caryl (oldest) was picking her college, we took a trip around several of the Texas colleges. I told her she could go anywhere she wanted but if the school was to be outside of Texas, it had to be because they had a special program in which she was interested. TCU was her choice. It is an excellent college. The same offer was given to each child. As each of the other children reached college age they applied to several schools, but even though they were accepted at other colleges as well, they all ended up going to TCU. I think that was somewhat of a record, as well as an endorsement of that school.

The Clinic grew both in numbers and stature, gaining even an international reputation for excellence in diagnosis and treatment of medical problems. I could not have enjoyed the practice more. The physicians who were my colleagues were all of the highest professional caliber and were so compatible. Each focused upon the best care for the patients. The administration took care of all the business hassles so we were free to practice pure medicine and were allowed part time teaching at either Baylor or University of Texas Medical schools. A new associate could progress to senior partner status in very few years. As a senior, income was shared equally regardless of the individual's gross as we looked at each subspecialty as equal.

All of the proper incentives were in place and working. Then the economics shifted. Our strength had always been in taking the time each patient required to get a full understanding of their problem. We routinely scheduled a full hour with a new patient, followed a few days later with a half hour appointment to discuss the results of our evaluation. As government and private insurance companies became the dominant payors for medical services, a procedure or special test requiring only a few minutes was reimbursed at several times what was paid for cognitive services. The result was that some physicians saw their gross double or triple compared to the others, and those with the highest gross started to leave the clinic. After several years of stability we saw a weakening rather than the strengthening we had expected. I always thought that the Clinic would become the Mayo Clinic of the south, a goal never reached. Nevertheless, my 30 years and 3 months were very rewarding, working with such a strong group of highly trained and motivated physicians.

Finally, Private Practice

During those years, I became very active in organized medicine, that is, in those professional societies which supported education and ethics of the profession. I served in many capacities, ultimately as the president of the Houston Society of Internal Medicine, the Texas Chapter of the American College of Physicians, the Texas Club of Internists, and the Harris County Medical Society. Jeanne was always at my side making attendance at social and professional meetings easy. She could remember names, faces, and details, and engage in conversation with anyone. Alone, I would have fumbled, but, with her at my side, I was confident and effective. Jeanne was, indeed," the wind under my wings".

Perhaps the high point in those activities was when, as president of the Harris County Medical Society, we received special recognition from President Ronald Reagan including an invitation to the White House.

As tensions over money increased at the clinic, I became increasingly uncomfortable. The focus on revenue seemed more important to some than excellence in service to our patients. The final straw to me was when the clinic voted to start advertising. That practice had always been deemed unethical for organized medicine until a Supreme Court decision decreed that advertising was nothing more than free speech. I was not convinced. I thought a physician's practice should be built upon his reputation for excellence, not on the strength of his or her advertising. I still feel that way and know that the public is not well served when they respond to ads—especially for professional services.

My discomfort with the direction the Clinic was taking reached its peak in 1989. At that same time I received a call from Kenneth Toppell, M.D., a pulmonologist who practiced at St. Joseph's Hospital which was downtown. I had known him since his residency and fellowship and considered him to be the best pulmonologist in the whole southwest. He told me that he was considering a move to Park Plaza Hospital where I was the Chief of the pulmonary service. I interpreted his call to be exploratory, trying to sense if there would be resistance to his move. I responded that it would be great to have him on the staff, and asked if there was anything I could do to make the move easier for him. He then asked if we could share night and weekend coverage. I told him the Clinic did not allow such agreements for many valid reasons relating to records, billing and legal considerations. He surprised me then by asking if there was any way we could get together as partners. I was overwhelmed. My unhappiness with the direction the Clinic was going and the possibility of practicing with someone I greatly admired made me very susceptible to such an offer.

We had a few exploratory meetings and soon realized that both our practices were too large, and that combining them would likely overwhelm us both. If a younger pulmonologist with a smaller practice were available to join us, then it could work. Nelson Fernandez. M.D. was that man, and thankfully he was interested. We moved forward with the details and the three of us planned to start a joint practice on January 1, 1990.

During these negotiations, however, I suffered a massive pulmonary embolus, one that nearly proved fatal. Jeanne and I had planned a trip to Malaysia and I was advised to take the typhoid immunization before we left. I did and had a severe febrile reaction to the shot. I was in bed for a couple of days, and then felt poorly the rest of the week. The following Monday, on Labor Day, 1989, I awakened a bit short of breath. It was worse with activity and we wondered if it might be psychological because of the stress of the impending change in my practice after over 30 years at the clinic.

When the shortness of breath worsened as I went out to get the newspaper, I felt that something was physically wrong. I called the clinic and found out that Nelson Fernandez was the doctor on call at the ER so we went in. Of course, the exam revealed nothing and the x-ray, EKG and blood tests were all normal as well. Nelson decided to do one more test. Since I was short of breath, he requested an arterial blood gas. The partial pressure of oxygen was very low, raising the suspicion of emboli. Then a radioisotope lung scan was done revealing many areas of the lungs with no circulation, diagnostic of multiple emboli. I was hospitalized and given the usual treatment of Heparin, an injectable anticoagulant, followed by the slower acting anticoagulant, oral Coumadin.

I seemed to improve rapidly and went home on Friday. My blood coagulation test on Saturday (done close to home) was right on the targeted therapeutic level. The next day, Sunday morning at 2 AM, I was awakened by sharp chest pain. I knew I was having more clots. We went back to the hospital where a Heparin IV was started. As I was lying in bed talking to Jeanne and my minister, I felt something hit me in the chest and I started to pass out. I called to Jeanne and asked her to "call a code" and passed out.

As the medical team worked on me, I was aware only of her voice. Jeanne remained at my side talking to me and holding the oxygen to my face. I am convinced that this contact with her was the real reason that I did not die. I saw only a bright white light similar to what has been described by many patients in near death circumstances and could hear her voice but nothing else. I teased her after my recovery by telling friends that she kept whispering in my ear, "Don't you dare die and leave me with this mortgage."

Actually she kept her cool and told me how much she loved me. You cannot even imagine what strength that gave me. I regained consciousness quickly and was taken to the ICU where I had another episode. By then many of my clinic partners had gathered around and consulted. Finally Nelson announced to me that they decided to try to get TPA (the clot buster tissue plasminogen activator) for me in the morning. TPA was still experimental and not approved for use in pulmonary emboli, but we knew enough about it to know that it was clearly indicated. I told Nelson not to wait for morning as I felt I would not still be alive then. It was started immediately and within an hour I was feeling better.

The next morning they placed a filter in my vena cava (main vein to the heart), thus preventing any new emboli from doing any serious damage. My lung scan rapidly improved. At its worst, the scan showed no circulation to my left lung and several large areas in my right lung. I felt well in just a few days. Nelson had to answer to a review committee for using TPA since it was not approved, even though it had saved my life. This episode brought back memories of the thrombophlebitis I had suffered as a complication of my episode of mumps with high fever when I was in the Air Force.

My recovery was so fast and so complete it did not alter our plans to move from the clinic to our three-man pulmonology practice at Park Plaza. My youngest daughter, Mary, was an audiologist and worked for an ENT group. She was in charge of their hearing center and was familiar with the operation of a physician's office. She told me that she would like to work for me in the new office. I had always had a registered nurse as my assistant but since we would have two RN's at the desk, I felt that she could handle it. Also we were very close and I knew her abilities. Very soon Mary was the one everyone turned to to get things done. She performed the pulmonary functions and EKG's, started the IV's, drew the arterial blood gasses, and did the chest x-rays right along with the nurses. These last six years of my medical practice with her as my assistant and Ken Toppell as my partner were the happiest of my career. The patients liked her so much that when I announced my retirement in December 1995, every single patient asked, "Is Mary quitting too?"

I think they thought that they could adjust to another doctor easier than to another doctor's assistant. She had such a way with them. They knew that if they were ill, Mary would get them in right away even if the schedule was already overloaded. If their situation was not urgent, she could still satisfy them by talking to them and setting up a later appointment or by telling them she would call if there was a cancellation. During this time Jeanne became second mother to our granddaughter Elyse (Mary's oldest), caring for her when Mary was at work with me. Later she also took care of Bryan (Mary's second) so that Mary could continue to work. Can you imagine how much work that was for a 63-70 year old whose health was still very fragile? But she did it with a smile and made it look easy and the children loved her more than ever.

Then near my 70th birthday I began to have health problems. On a routine checkup, a cancer of the prostate was discovered. I decided on radiation therapy instead of surgery, partly because of my history of clots. The therapy was very difficult and about halfway through it I wanted to stop. Jeanne insisted that I complete it, all 7000 rads, and I did. Now, almost 14 years later, I still suffer significant side effects of the radiation but have had no recurrence of the cancer. Then I developed aseptic necrosis of my right hip forcing me to consider a total hip replacement. This convinced me that it was time to retire. We set December 31, 1995, as my last day and Mary's as well. She returned to her role as a full time mom and I began the uncertain future of retirement.

9

Laughter Really Is The Best Medicine

Some of the funniest incidents in my lifetime seem worthy of recording even though these jokes are aimed directly at me. (I am, after all, human and can be allowed a few weaknesses.) I believe that if you can't laugh at yourself, you shouldn't laugh at anyone else, either. So here you go: these laughs are on me.

THE BUNNY STORY

When I got out of the Air Force in 1959, we bought a house on the southwest side of Houston in a subdivision named Westbury which was an ideal place for the children to play, with a large backyard and a swimming pool.

Once we were settled the children were anxious to have pets and they especially wanted rabbits so we built a hutch behind the garage and got two white domestic rabbits. They did, indeed, turn out to be easy to care for and play with. Since the yard was fenced, they were often let out of the hutch to roam the yard during the day but, to avoid predators, they were always to be in the hutch at night. On a couple of occasions, they were left out but the children would catch them and put them back in the hutch.

In those days, emergency rooms were not staffed by a physician so when an emergency call came, I would jump in the car and go to the hospital emergency center to give care. Early one morning, about 2:30 AM, I received a call from one of my patients who had rather frequent attacks of pulmonary edema (heart failure). I called the ER and gave them orders to start treatment if the patient arrived before I did, then quickly dressed and jumped in the car. About a half block from the house, I saw one of the rabbits in a neighbor's flower bed.

I knew the children would be heartbroken if she was lost and that I had plenty of time to get to the ER before the patient, so I got out of the car and tried to grab the rabbit. She was particularly hard to catch and I rather trampled the flowers, but I finally threw my white coat over her and caught her and put her into the back seat. By then I felt that I did not have time to take the rabbit back to the hutch, so I left her in the car with the plan to let the children clean up any mess as punishment for letting her out. I still got to the ER about the same time as my patient, and was able to stabilize him and get him admitted to the hospital for further treatment.

When I arrived home, it was about 5:30 AM, too late to go back to bed. So I showered, shaved and dressed for work as the children also prepared for breakfast and school.

When they came to the table it was clear to the children that I was tired and grumpy because of lack of sleep, so there was almost no conversation. I gave them a stern look and loudly commanded that they go out and check the rabbits. They asked why, but I just repeated my order. They were gone about 5 minutes and then quietly came in and slipped into their chairs at the table without saying anything. I waited a couple minutes and growled, "WELL?"

They replied, "Well what, daddy?" to which I said, "Well, how are the rabbits?" They said in unison, "They are fine, daddy."

There was a long pause as I let that sink in. Then, in a softer voice this time, I told them to go out and check the back seat of the car. They complied, and came in holding the rabbit that I had caught on the way to the hospital, asking "Can we keep him daddy?"

Only then was I sure that I had caught someone else's pet rabbit. I felt lucky that I hadn't been shot at as a prowler. When the children came home from school, they went from door to door to find the new rabbit's rightful owner, less than a block away. But that wasn't the end of the story. It turned out that the neighbor's rabbit was a male and our two rabbits were females. And yes, in a few weeks we did have a bunch of little rabbits.

SOUNDS IN THE NIGHT

One night, shortly after going to bed but before I was fully asleep, Jeanne reached over and shook my shoulder and asked, "Joel, did you hear that noise?" I had not heard anything but she was clearly concerned, so I got up and walked through the house checking, as carefully as I could, for anything moving or out of place. I looked through all the windows as well, seeing nothing strange. The children had not been awakened. I reassured her that all was okay and that we should go to sleep.

Only moments later, Jeanne again pushed on my shoulder and said "There it is again." She did not recognize the sound as anything she had ever heard before and couldn't describe it to me.

Again, I got up and searched the house, putting on all the lights both inside the house and in the yard as well. I could find nothing out of the ordinary, so again I reassured Jeanne, and, leaving all the lights on for the feeling of security that they provided, tried again to sleep.

Before I dozed off, suddenly all the lights went out, both inside and outside the house. Now, we were both frightened and thought someone had pulled the main electric switch outside the house with undoubtedly evil intentions. I didn't call the police however, because in those days it took an hour or two for police to respond to any thing that did not really qualify as an emergency.

I had no weapons of any kind in the house as I had always felt that they posed a much greater threat to inquisitive children than to a potential criminal. But I did have my father's ceremonial Shriners' sword tucked away in a closet. (It had no sharp edges or points but did look threatening.) I took it and a flashlight and looked through the house, now for a third time. Finding nothing, I screwed up my courage, and went out to check the main light switch, waving the sword viciously to frighten away any intruders. I am sure that anyone seeing me in my short pajama bottoms, waving the sword and shining the flashlight in all directions would have died laughing.

The breaker box was indeed open. Then I remembered that we had an electric short in one of the waterfall pumps and had been careful not to turn it on. When I turned on all the lights, I had turned it on without thinking, and after a few minutes, it had caused the blackout.

We still had no idea what the strange noises had been but, by now, we were so wide awake, we just sat and talked. Then the noise recurred. This time, I heard it as well and was able to trace it to a tree branch that was rubbing the roof right over our bedroom at any slight breeze.

We still laugh at how silly I must have looked, defending our home in the dead of night in my shorty pajamas, wielding a useless weapon.

TANDEM BIKING

Our Westbury neighborhood was a good place to live and raise our five children, but it was not the best place to bicycle because of too many busy intersections and too much traffic.

Jeanne never learned to ride a bike growing up in Chicago, because her father feared the traffic, so in Houston we rode a tandem bicycle. She rode in the rear seat and I controlled the bike up front. When the weather would allow, we biked almost daily, usually several miles. Braes Bayou had a nice bike trail which we used while we were in Westbury, and once we moved to the Woodlands our favorite biking trail was a wooded nature trail with many of the native flora species labeled much like an arboretum. Along this route we could relax, enjoying nature and freely flowing conversation. We really enjoyed this time together away from phones or other interruptions for an hour or more, at the same time getting our exercise. The Woodlands was an ideal place for biking with over 50 miles of trails, many parks and almost no traffic. It was like living in a small town out in the country, and was almost an hour closer to the lake where we spent many of our week-ends. Although it was considerably further from my work, these benefits made the extra commuting time tolerable.

One day as we started out on our bike ride Jeanne rested her head on my back and sighed. I remembered that she had said earlier in the day that she didn't feel up to par. I said "We don't have to bike today," I said. "Let's go home."

She insisted that she was all right and promised to tell me if she wanted to shorten the ride or quit. So off we went, our pace a little slower than usual. We decided to go on the nature trail that day, a route that required crossing one major street at a stoplight. At the light I shifted the gears and in so doing jammed them. We got off the bike and I fixed the chain easily. As soon as the light changed, I started off again. I had gone about a mile when I realized that Jeanne wasn't talking much, and I feared that she was feeling worse but just wouldn't tell me. When I looked over my shoulder to check on her I panicked. She was gone! Was I talking so much that she could have fainted and fallen off the bike without my noticing? I quickly reversed course, looking to both sides of the trail for her. At one point, shifting gears for a hill, I again jammed them. Only a few feet away, there was a single golfer on a cart. I yelled to him that I had an emergency and needed his cart. He obligingly got off and turned the cart over to me. Now I could retrace my path much faster.

Even with the cart, I could not find Jeanne. I struggled to remember when I had last heard her speak to me and drove to that spot but she was not there. I rushed to a nearby house and asked if they had seen a lady wandering about, but they had not. The homeowner suggested that we call the sheriff, and I did. He responded in less than two minutes, suggesting that I get in the police car with him and that we drive around the neighborhood looking for her. We did, but still, no Jeanne. My panic was increasing. Finally the sheriff asked where I lived. I gave him the address and we drove toward home.

When we were almost there, I spotted Jeanne walking slowly toward home. I leaped out of the car and ran to her asking, "What happened.... how are you . . . are you hurt?"

Her response? "Oh, Joel! Don't you remember when we got off the bike at the traffic light? You rode off before I could get back on." When I asked why she didn't call out to stop me, she answered, "I just couldn't believe you didn't know that I was not there. By the time I realized you didn't miss me, you were out of earshot."

The sheriff said, "You two had better tie yourselves together with a rope." Then he drove us back to the house where we had abandoned the borrowed golf cart. The homeowner had already taken the golf cart back to the clubhouse and also fixed the chain on our bike. What a good neighbor!

On the way home from our little adventure, Jeanne said, "I won't go out on that bike again till you paint it another color," no doubt hoping people wouldn't recognize us as the ditzy couple who lost each other on a bike ride.

Later that evening, we were aware of the sheriff driving by the house, probably on his routine rounds. Jeanne, though, thought he might be looking to see where those crazy people live. On my birthday, Mary, our youngest daughter gave me a rear view mirror for the bike. And we kept biking in spite of this incident, especially along the nature trail.

OH, JOEL!

"Oh, Joel!" was an oft-used expression of Jeanne's with many meanings. It could be interpreted as "I told you so" or "What in the world were you thinking?", or simply "Why?". Nowhere was it more fitting than when she used it in this setting.

For many years we had a cabin on Lake Livingston as our weekend getaway. I had purchased the land even before the dam was completed and we started building before the water had reached the shoreline.

A patient of mine, Bob Aberson, who was a pilot for one of the oil companies and thus travelled extensively, had also purchased land in the same development. In his travels, Bob had visited a company that made cedar home kits. By kit, I mean that much of the tongue and groove cedar came already cut to length, making construction much easier and faster. In addition, the manufacturer would send an engineer-carpenter with the kit to supervise the assembly at what we both thought was a bargain rate. The company wanted to penetrate the Lake Livingston area market, and there would be a considerable saving for us if we both bought kits and had them shipped together. We agreed to proceed and I made some modifications to one of their standard designs. I wanted the whole front of the cabin to be glass so that there was a great view of the lake.

Our kits arrived on the same flatbed 18 wheeler. We took two weeks off work and with the help of the engineer-carpenter and two local carpenters we were able to complete the shells of both houses in the two weeks we had allowed. Our plans were to complete the inside finishing, electrical, plumbing, and air conditioning on our own as our individual schedules allowed.

Bob's schedule was much more flexible than mine but the private practice of medicine kept me pretty tied down except for the weekends I was not on call. Things were moving so slowly, I hired the skilled people to complete the job except the cabinetry which I could manage. We went to the cabin almost every chance we had and enjoyed boating, water skiing, fishing, sailing in our 16 foot Dolphin sailboat, napping in the hammock, and lots of playing games with the children.

As the children grew up and had their own families, some moving far away as their jobs demanded, we found ourselves using the cabin only on special occasions or holidays such as the Fourth of July, Labor Day, etc. Maintenance went on as usual and the place finally became more of a chore for Jeanne and me than a playground for the whole family, as well as a significant financial drain. There are a million happy tales to tell about the fun days at the cabin but the funniest one is the one I want to tell here.

We made the very hard decision that we must sell the cabin rather than keep up the expense of maintenance, and the work that was needed each time we did go there. Because I wanted to bring the boat home to store it nearby where I could work on it as needed and clean it up for sale, I had loaded it on the trailer and parked it on the lot which I also owned next to the cabin. Before we left, however, a heavy rainstorm saturated the ground. I still felt that I could pull the boat and trailer out with our pickup truck and bring it home, but all thought otherwise, especially Jeanne, who wanted me to leave it till another time. I was determined to at least try and asked everyone to get in back and push as I started to pull it out of the mud with the truck.

Well, as all but me expected, the truck and trailer didn't move an inch, but the wheels spun wildly spraying large volumes of mud. Everyone behind the truck got at least somewhat muddy, but Jeanne, who was right behind the spinning wheels, was completely covered from the top of her head to the tips of her toes. When she opened her eyes, one could see the whites but everything else was mud.

Her only words before she walked down and jumped in the lake were **"Oh, Joel!"** and I think this time they meant "Stupid."

SAILING

We kept a small centerboard sailboat at the lake cottage. It was 16 feet long and was called a Dolphin. The children all learned to sail in it and the stronger the wind and taller the waves, the more they enjoyed it. I think they especially like to tip it over and then right it. One person could easily bring it back upright.

On one of our trips to Grand Cayman, Jeanne and I rented a sunfish, a slightly smaller boat than our Dolphin. The weather was beautiful and there was a soft breeze blowing. We avoided the strong winds—after all, this boat was for relaxation, not racing. We sailed back and forth not far from the shore of seven mile beach, looking at the condominiums from a different vantage point. The sun was intense so we were both well covered with suntan lotion.

We had only been out for a little while when we passed near an overturned catamaran whose sole occupant was trying desperately to right it. It was too large and heavy for a single person to turn so I called to him and asked if he would like some help, which he welcomed. I let our sail loose and told Jeanne to stay with the Sunfish and I would swim over to him and help.

Jeanne was sitting on the side of the small cockpit and when I jumped in, the sunfish overturned. I asked her to stay with it since I would be right back. With the two of us, it took only a moment or two to get the other fellow upright and sailing away.

I got back to the sunfish and quickly righted it, crawling aboard to help Jeanne back in the boat. She was covered with suntan oil and was so slippery that she simply could not get aboard. Each time she tried she would come close but then slip back in the water. After several unsuccessful attempts, I told her to hold the rope and I would sail to the shore pulling her behind. We made it, but not without another **"Oh, Joel!"** This time it no doubt had several meanings, but "stupid" had to be at the top of the list.

THE ELECTRIC ORGAN

Our brother-in-law George Miller is a research scientist and quite knowledgeable about all things electronic. He was excited when the transistor was developed and became readily available. It apparently had many applications none of which I understood, but George felt that it would be ideal for an electronic organ. It sounded like a lot of fun and we were sure the children would love to play with it more than with a toy piano, so we got the idea that we should make one for them. All we would need was a speaker, various resistors, a transistor, a soldering iron, and a keyboard. We found a small toy piano in a toy store. This was the kind that looked like a small grand piano and had about 8 keys. These keys struck iron bars that looked like a comb and issued a tinkle which varied with the length of the specific iron bar.

George assured me that this was exactly what we wanted and that we could use the existing iron bars as resistors because the resistance would be in proportion to the length of the bar. We could position the point where we soldered the wire to the transistor at the point where the sound was the best and adjust it till we had a scale of notes.

We labored to get the transistor wired to the bars and to the speaker and finally had everything hooked up to give a different note when each key was depressed. We were so proud of ourselves and even had ideas of grandeur that we could market the idea.

Everyone gathered around for the concert. The sound came out as squeaks and not very pretty ones at that. Our faces dropped and our audience only laughed. We also had a good laugh and decided to keep our day jobs.

"DO IT AGAIN, DADDY!"

Just before the Christmas of 1951, Jeanne and I and daughter Caryl (then 34 months old) were living in Toledo, Ohio, where I was stationed by the Air Force in a recruiting and induction station. Jeanne's sister and her husband were still in college in Albion, Michigan, and we had a few days off for the holiday. We decided that it would be nice to drive to Chicago and spend the Christmas holiday with the girls' parents and grandparents. We planned to drive the 60 miles to Albion, pick up Jeanne's sister and brother-in-law, and then drive another 150 miles to Chicago. This would normally be a four or five hour drive. Any planned travel at that time of year has the risk of bad weather and sure enough the evening before we were to leave a heavy snowstorm hit. We felt that we were experienced in driving in winter weather, so off we went. The closer we got to Albion, the worse the road conditions became. Still we thought that we could turn south to a highway with better road conditions. The first westbound highway we came to turned out to be no better. We went further south. The snow had partially melted to slush, but refrozen so that it was rough, so rough it would turn the car. We saw a highway patrolman and asked if there was a better route but he just advised us to find a motel for the night. We had been on the road nearly 10 hours and were not even halfway to our destination. We saw big 18 wheelers way off the highway in fields where they had lost control and slid to a stop. We continued driving, trying to find a motel with a room available. Our speed was less than 15 miles per hour.

All of a sudden, even at that slow speed, the car started sliding, rotating 270 degrees and then sliding off the highway rear end first into the ditch. We were all very frightened except young Caryl, who shouted, "Do it again, Daddy!" She was laughing and clapping her hands. We laughed at that but wondered how we would be able to get out of the ditch.

The next car to come along was a Model A Ford with an elderly farm woman behind the wheel. She jumped out of her car and grabbed a shovel from her back seat and started shoveling before we could stop her. We asked her to let us borrow her shovel and let us do the work. She refused and told us to get behind and push, and for one of the wives to drive. In about five minutes we were back on the highway, most grateful to this caring and capable lady.

We pulled in to the next motel, staying in their lobby with several other travelers. In the morning, the sun came out and the icy road became drivable. We reached home in Chicago 28 hours after we left Toledo, and had learned our lesson to never drive on ice.

DON'T DO THIS UNLESS YOU CAN FLY!

Houston is very humid and molds and mildew thrive in the city's moist atmosphere. They grow best in wet, dark places or shaded areas, and can be seen in a variety of colors. When they appear on the exterior of the house, even a paint that is still in good condition can look pretty bad. Every few years it becomes necessary to clean up the painted surface to brighten up the house. Usually a mixture of chlorine and water is sufficient and does a fairly good job at very little expense. But the results don't last very long before the cleaning has to be done again.

I searched the internet for an alternative and found many possibilities. Some were harmful to nearby plants; others were fairly toxic and best applied by a professional. I did, however, find one that sounded especially appropriate for me, an amateur at this sort of thing. It was moderately expensive but promised to last several years if applied properly.

The technique was to use a pressure sprayer to apply the treatment to the surface, allow it to penetrate for about 30 minutes and then rinse it off gently. (Not really a thorough rinse, but enough to make the surface look clear.) This all seemed simple enough so I bought the appropriate amount to treat the total exterior of the house, gathered the tools (pressure sprayer, ladder, and hose), and proceeded to the roof of our attached garage so that I could reach the highest point of the house with the spray.

Standing on the peak of the roof with one foot on one side of the ridge and the other foot on the other side, I felt very stable and safe. The job went smoothly and it took only a few minutes to apply the chemical. When I was done I put the sprayer aside and tried to turn to reach the hose.

The roof was made of wooden shingles and the chemical, which had run down on them, made the surface icy slick. I couldn't move either foot without starting to slide. It was clear that I needed help.

I called out to Jeanne who was inside the house but she could not hear me. I shouted, screamed, and pounded on the wall trying to get her attention or that of a neighbor. No luck. I was stuck until someone came within earshot which was about a half hour later when Jeanne came out to see how I was progressing with the job. When she saw my dilemma we discussed the possibilities. She could call the fire department and ask them to bring the hook and ladder truck. I thought that would be too embarrassing and might possibly make the local newspaper, fully exposing my stupidity. We joked that though I felt I was very high up, clearly it was not high enough for a parachute. We were having a good laugh even, though I knew the situation could result in injury.

I decided that if we had a rope long enough, we could tie it on a tree on one side of the garage, pass it over the top, and drop the end on the other side. I could then let myself down slowly and safely. But we had nothing long enough. So I asked Jeanne to go the nearest hardware store and get 100 feet of rope, strong enough to hold my weight (160 lbs.)

Then I not too patiently waited about 30 minutes for her return. Jeanne had not been a Girl Scout and knew little about tying knots. Nevertheless she tied the rope to the designated tree with a series of granny knots and then tried to throw the rope up to me. She was unable. It was quite high up and I couldn't move. We decided that I would lower the end of the hose to her and she could tie the free end of the rope to it. That worked and I was able to pull the rope up to me and lower the end to the other side of the house.

When I made it down with no injuries except to my pride, I received strict orders from Jeanne that I was never to go on the roof again, but to leave that to the professionals. Incidentally, the mold and mildew stuff worked very well, and we had no problems for several years.

But, there was still another **"Oh, Joel!"**

THE MOUNTAIN CLIMBERS—NOT!

One more **"Oh, Joel!"** bears telling. While George and Caryl were in Lafayette, Indiana, and Jeanne and I were in Indianapolis during my residency, George got an invitation for us all to go to a lakeside lodge in northern Canada. We arranged our vacation time so that we could go together. I believe the place was called White Lake, and it was far enough north that we had to register with the Mounties and give them our planned itinerary and timetable.

This was quite a place. There were only two residences on the lake which was very large. The lodge was luxurious. There was a main cabin and two or three smaller guest cabins, a boat, and everything we could possibly need. We hiked and boated around the lake, but no swimming—the water was far too cold. The only inconvenience was that it was June which meant black fly season. The flies were numerous and when they landed on your skin, they immediately left a sore which took weeks to heal and itched intensely. We couldn't stand still and looked like we were doing some sort of dance as we tried to cope with them. If we went fast enough in the boat we would get away from them for awhile.

Jeanne and I slept in one of the guest cabins perhaps 30 feet away from the main lodge. One night we heard noises at the door and peeked out to see a very large grizzly bear. When we felt sure that he was gone, we raced into the main lodge. We never saw him again but kept a wary eye.

On the far side of the lake the terrain rose almost straight up. There was a good amount of vegetation but it was rocky and climbing didn't seem to be too much of a challenge. George and I decided to try to climb to the top. We had no experience in rock climbing but had seen it done in movies and on TV. It didn't impress us as being too hard. We knew that the experts used ropes and other equipment but the only thing we had was a rope. We tied one end to me and the other end to him and started up. George was in the lead and reached about the top one third when he called back to me that he could not advance further and that we should go back down. Only then did we learn that going down was way harder than going up. We realized that the rope between us only assured that if one fell, the other would be dragged down as well, since the rope was not secured to anything except each other. When we finally made it back to the bottom we decided that we were not mountain climbers. Jeanne's comment: **"Oh, Joel!"**

The Jung Family 1883

The Belgenland

Carl (Bobo) & Augusta (Gussie)

Robert and Edna Vogel

George, Caryl, Jeanne and me

Caryl, Jennifer, Megan and Jeanne ~ Four Generations of First Daughters

Vogel Home at 8132 S. Ada Street, Chicago

Calumet High School

Vogel Home at 532 S. Park Rd., La Grange

Cottage on Scott Lake

1942 ~ She loved to swim.

My parents, Joel Sr. and Gladys

The Woodward children
Standing (l-r) Florence, Ethel, Roswell
Seated, Harold, Gladys (my mother)

Me in 1943

Wesley Memorial Hospital

Abbott Hall Med Student residence

Hampshire House Nursing Student Residence

Northwestern university Med School

1947 Aircoupe

The Methodist Church in Tucson

The Wedding Chapel

Mom, Jeanne & I with 1936 Ford

Our Wedding Photograph

Punta Penasca Mexico 1948

Our First Car 1936 Ford

Med school was hard work

On the way to the Philippines

MSTS Barrett

Our Philippine Home

Tropical Paradise

Teaching Nursing in the Philippines

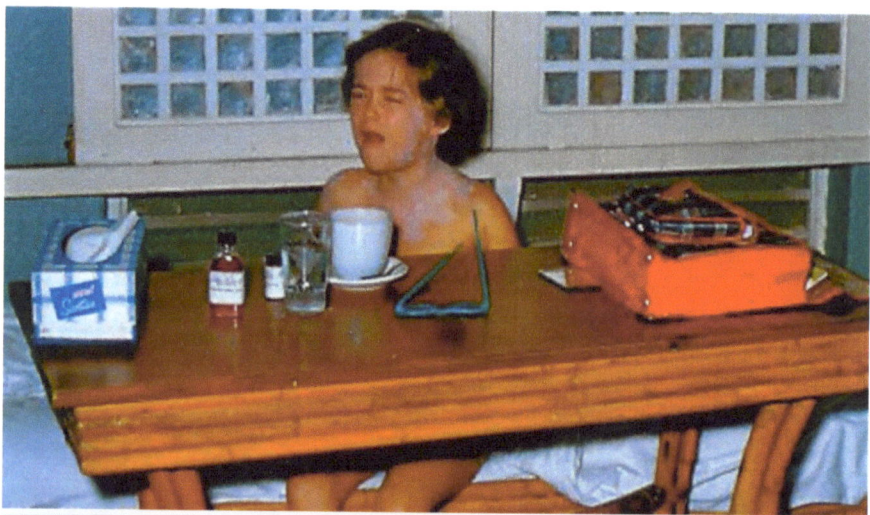

Caryls Measles

5131 Hummingbird St.

Diagnostic Clinic 1959

Diagnostic Clinic 1985

Diagnostic Clinic & Hospital 1985

Hermann Hospital 1959

Lake Livingston Cottage

The Lake

22 Bracken Fern Ct.

My shop

The Sunfish

My First Office

Jeanne, Cadet Nurse Corps 1944

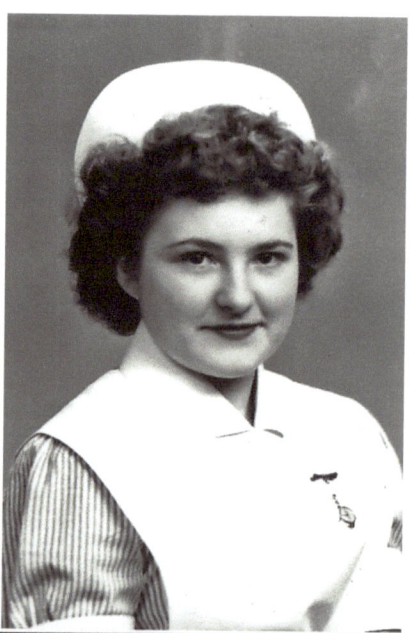
Jeanne Student Nurse 1945

Mudbath

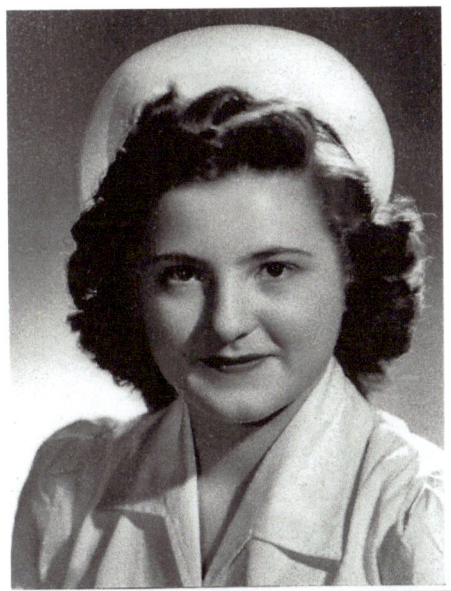

Jeanne Registered Nurse 1945

Jeanne

Jeanne's Sewing

She made one for each grandchild

Jeanne's Painting

Those busy hands

With Pres. Reagan & V.P. Bush 1984

Family Photo 1998

The Memories Quilt 1997

The Calendar, A Gift From Jeanne Miller ~ 1997

Gift made by our girls

50th Reunion at Lake Arbutus

Family Tree, designed by Jeanne Miller

Working in the Community Clinic

Grand Canyon 1955

Parasailing Mexico

China - She loved the children

Great Barrier Reef

Sting Ray City, Grand Cayman

Whitewater rafting Canada

Don't ever tell Jeanne that she physically can't do something. She made it to the top of the great wall.

Great Wall of China 1984

Snowshoeing in the Rockies

Dinner on the QE2

Venice 2007

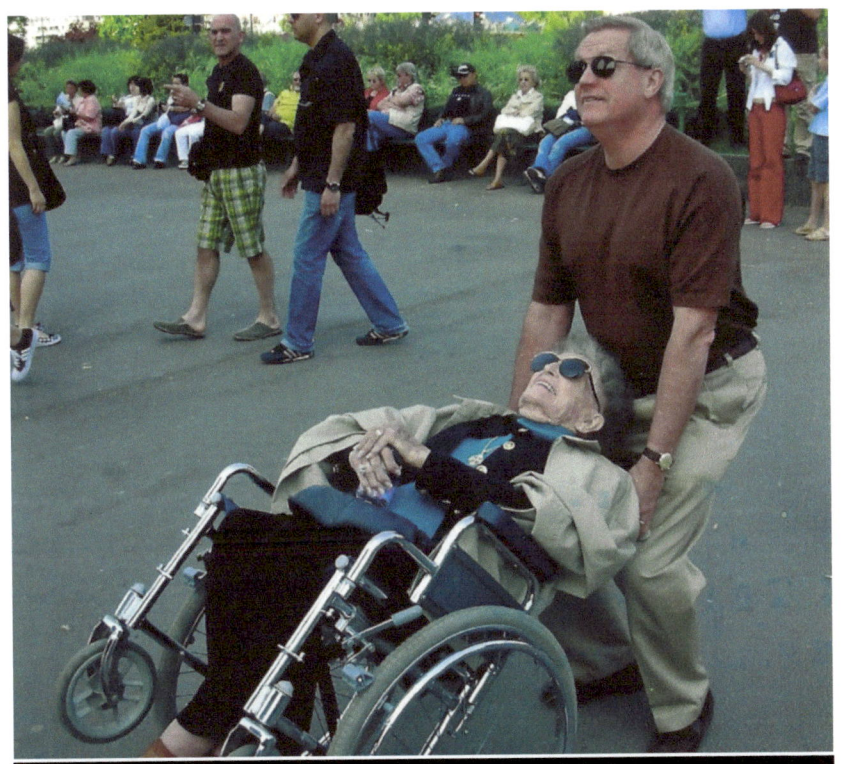
Viewing the Eiffel Tower 2007

Hong Kong 1996

First Catch

60th Anniversary

Kauai

Yosemite 2007

Jeanne and I in upper left, Jerusalem with friends

10

Jeanne

What made this woman so remarkable? What about her had such a profound effect on so many people? Why was she so loved by everyone who knew her? How did she spread her faith to so many without saying a word? What is her legacy?

Jeanne was the sort of person who had an immediate impact on everyone she met. This was certainly true of me. She literally bowled me over with her beauty, intelligence, and conversational skill at our first meeting. I always considered her the best conversationalist I had ever met. My thesaurus says the word "conversationalist" means a talker, communicator, or chatterbox. Encarta defines it as "somebody who enjoys engaging in conversation and can converse in an enjoyable way." Certainly communicator is an accurate synonym, but it has taken my whole lifetime to learn that it is not the **talker** who is a conversationalist but the **listener**.

When I learned this I had the opportunity to ask my 16 year old grandson, "What makes a good conversationalist?" Without hesitation he answered "listening." I am sure that he learned that from Jeanne, not because she told him so, but because he had observed her. Listening was one of Jeanne's strong points and one of the reasons so may were attracted to her and learned to love her so quickly. She really listened, and I don't mean just hearing. She listened intently and remembered everything (so much so, we always teased her that she had the memory of an elephant), and she did it with so much sensitivity that in mere moments she learned more about the other person than most learn after a long friendship.

Her sincere interest in a person, their family, work, and their personal likes and dislikes was immediately apparent. When she next saw them, even years later, she would amaze them with her recall as she asked questions about the most minute details. Naturally, they felt a real connection with her. She loved everyone and they could sense this. If anyone, family or friend had a problem; she found a way to guide the conversation so that they could see the solution or at least the approach that would lead to resolution. I told her many times that had she gone to medical school instead of nursing school, she would have been the greatest psychiatrist of all time. Freud and Jung and the other greats would have had to play second fiddle to my Jeanne.

Jeanne was raised in the Lutheran Church, Missouri Synod, but had no problem in changing to the Lutheran Church in America (now the

Evangelical Lutheran Church in America) when I had concerns about some of the Missouri Synod's fundamentalist ideas. I think the two things that bothered me the most were their restrictions on serving communion, and the place of women in the governance of the congregations. We both felt that we should worship together in the same church and that such unity was important to the whole family.

Neither Jeanne nor I pushed religion on the children. We went to church regularly and they accompanied us. I do not ever recall any resistance to that; it was just part of our routine. A friend once asked Jeanne "How do you get your children to go to church every Sunday?" Jeanne responded with a question of her own: "How do you get yours to go to school?" Our children seemed to look forward to both church and school.

We participated in many church sponsored activities and the children did as well, including Sunday school, sports, camps and even jobs on committees, etc. Every one of them remains very active in their church to this day, and the grandchildren are as well. It was In this nurturing environment that our children learned the virtuous thoughts and actions which they would never be exposed to on the streets.

Jeanne accomplished this legacy purely by example and by the joyous way she approached life and religion in general. So many of her friends and former Sunday school students have expressed to me what a great impact her life and example had on them. She touched so many lives and all were the better for it.

Just a few weeks after Jeanne's death, the drama group at our church acted out a skit designed to retain and enlist Sunday school teachers. The setting was the church office, with the secretary at the desk. A teacher came in asking for the Pastor but he was not there at the time. So, the teacher explained that the reason for his visit was to resign as a teacher, feeling that he was not doing a good job keeping up with the lesson plans and was therefore ineffective. As he was talking with the secretary a young lady came in and recognized him as her Sunday school teacher years before. She praised him and said that he had been a powerful force in her younger years and had influenced her whole life.

I sat in the pew and broke out in tears as a few days earlier I had received a condolence card with a contribution to one of Jeanne's charities from an adult who had been in one of her classes many years ago when she had been a Sunday school teacher. This woman wrote in her card to me almost word for word the dialogue from the drama group's presentation. She shared what a powerful force Jeanne's teachings had been and how they had influenced her life. It makes one wonder about coincidences.

As busy and hectic as the Reed household was with five children ranging in age from a few months to 11 years, Jeanne still found time for many activities. Her hands were never still whether it was reading, knitting, sewing, needle pointing, painting (toll painting), or teaching Sunday school.

And best of all, she made it all look easy. She needle pointed uniquely designed Christmas stockings for each of the twelve grandchildren. Each one is a museum-quality piece and they will last as heirlooms for many generations.

Her family members were not the only ones who loved her. When I returned to work after Jeanne's death at the Community Clinic where she volunteered as a receptionist and I as a physician for over 10 years, I got a very warm reception with many hugs and expressions of shared grief. Becky, our laboratory technician, gave me a big hug and said, "See, I'm wearing my pin." Then Lee said the same, showing me that she had hers on as well. They were beautiful three-dimensional hearts with a stone which looked like a diamond set in the center. I asked about their significance, and they responded, "Don't you know?"

I answered "no."

They went on to explain that an anonymous donor provided the funds to purchase a pin for each volunteer at the clinic "in memory of Jeanne." They had been distributed at the annual volunteer dinner a few days before. I had not attended, so it was a surprise to me. It further demonstrated how very much everyone loved and respected my angel Jeanne.

I have tried to think of the adjectives which best describe Jeanne. There are so many and I couldn't choose between them. Adjectives like loving, affectionate, tender, fond, devoted, amorous, kind, compassionate, benevolent, humane, caring, sympathetic, nice, gentle, patient, enduring, tolerant, uncomplaining, long suffering, serene, giving, charitable, philanthropic, generous, listening, considerate, concerned, sensitive, thoughtful, and helpful.

I am sure that there are many others, too, but these are the most obvious to me. I have been warned that it is often the case for a husband or wife to place a deceased spouse upon a pedestal, but I can assure you that these pedestal-placing thoughts long preceded Jeanne's death, and are confirmed by those who knew her best. It is no wonder that she was loved so much by so many and no wonder why I grieve her loss so intensely. She was truly God's masterpiece.

Twelve years ago, at our 50th anniversary celebration, our niece Jeanne Miller gave us a calendar where each one of 365 pages contained a statement from a family member in response to a question asked of them. This calendar is a treasure and one of the most thoughtful gifts the two of us ever received. It must have taken countless hours of loving care and work to put together. I still turn a page each day and read the entries with gratitude. The whole calendar is much too much to include here but some of the entries give an insight into the effect Jeanne had on family:

> "Grandmother taught me sincerity, patience, love. The list could go on and on. My grandma is such a real person. In everything she does, you can see her true love for others. Never have I heard her raise her voice in anger. Never have I

heard her take credit for her kind actions, even when they are due. And I have never seen her put herself before another. I try everyday to remember these qualities and make them more a part of who I am." *Granddaughter Jennifer Zucconi*

"The thing I admire most about Mom is her patience. She keeps the family balanced". *Daughter Ann Reed Hopkinson*

"My most moving memory of Jeanne is one day, she said, 'Can I just call you my daughter because you are so special and daughter-in-law just doesn't seem right anymore.' Of course, I said yes!" *John's wife Lisa Reed*

"One thing I admire about Mom is her patience and strength, and her ability to always see the good in situations where others tend to see the bad." *Caryl Reed Reese*

There are 361 more entries, but to read them all you must see the calendar for yourself.

The bottom line is that Jeanne lived her whole life with love as her guide. She truly loved her neighbor as herself and was humble, willing to give of herself whenever there was a need. She completely embodied the following words of God, and many more not listed.

Proverbs 31 The one thing I admire most about Jeanne:

"A wife of noble character who can find?
She is worth far more than rubies.

Her husband has full confidence in her
And lacks nothing of value.
She brings him good not harm,
All the days of her life.
She opens her arms to the poor
And extends her hands to the needy.
She speaks with wisdom and faithful instruction
Is on her tongue.
Her children arise and call her blessed;
Her husband also, and he praises her.
. . . a woman who fears the Lord should be
    praised.
Give her the reward she has earned."

I think that pretty much says it all.
                       Mary's husband Bill Jones

Philippians 2: 1-5: "If you have any encouragement from being united with Christ, if any comfort from His love, if any fellowship with the Spirit, if any tenderness and compassion, then make my joy complete by being like-minded, having the same love, being one in spirit and purpose. Do nothing out of selfish ambition or vain conceit, but in humility consider others better than yourselves. Each of you should look not only to your own interests, but also to the interests of others. Your attitude should be the same as that of Christ Jesus."

1Corinthians 13: 1-13: "And now I will show you the most excellent way. If I speak in tongues of men and of angels, but have not love, I am only a resounding gong or a clanging cymbal. If I have the gift of prophesy and can fathom all mysteries and all knowledge, and if I have a faith that can move mountains, but have not love, I am nothing. If I give all I possess to the poor and surrender my body to the flames, but have not love, I gain nothing. Love is patient, love is kind. It does not envy, it does not boast, it is not proud. It is not rude, it is not self-seeking, it is not easily angered, it keeps no record of wrongs. Love does not delight in evil but rejoices with the truth. It always protects, always trusts always hopes, always perseveres. Love never fails. But where there are prophesies, they will cease; where there are tongues, they will be stilled; where there is knowledge, it will pass away. For we know in part and we prophesy in part, but when perfection comes, the imperfect disappears. When I was a child, I reasoned like a child. When I became a man, I put childish ways behind me. Now we see but a poor reflection in a mirror; then we shall see face to face. Now I know in part; then I shall know fully, even as I am fully known. And now these three remain: faith, hope and love. But the greatest of these is love."

1 John 3: 18: "Dear children, let us not love with words or tongue but with actions and truth."

Matthew 25: 40: "The King will reply, "I tell you the truth, whatever you did for one of the least of these brothers of mine, you did for me."

John 3: 34-35: "A new command I give you: Love one another. As I have loved you, so you must love one another."

Romans 13: 9: "Whatever other commandments there may be, are summed up in this one rule: Love your neighbor as yourself."

Galatians 6: 2: "Carry each other's burdens, and in this way you will fulfill the law of Christ."

What a legacy Jeanne leaves: five wonderful children with spouses she loved as her if they were her own, twelve grandchildren, two with spouses she also considered her own, and three great granddaughters. I only hope they can comprehend the depth and intensity of the love she had for each one of them and how much she respected them for their individuality and character. All of them lead Christ-centered and family centered lives and they all love one another.

I thank God every day for the years He gave us together and look forward to being together in whatever the afterlife brings. Jesus referred to it as paradise, so it must be great. I felt life with Jeanne as my partner was paradise. A friend sent me an e-mail message just the other day and it pretty well defines my feelings. "A man was not feeling well and went to his physician for an examination. The doctor examined the patient thoroughly and did a few tests. Then he brought the man into his office and asked him to sit down.

"I am afraid I have bad news," he told the patient. "You have a cancer which has already spread. There is no really effective treatment available."

The patient responded "Doctor, I am afraid to die. Can you tell me what is on the other side?"

The doctor said, "I don't know."

"But," the man replied, "You are a Christian man and should have an idea at least."

Just then a scratching and whining noise came from the other side of the door. He opened the door and his dog raced in and joyfully jumped up on him. The doctor turned to the patient and said," It must be like my dog here. He had never been in this room before but he knew his master was here so he had no fear, just joy."

Again, I refer the reader to the calendar and its many entries about Jeanne, whose nicknames included My Special Angel, Superwoman, Wonderwoman, and God's Masterpiece. She was, indeed, the perfect wife and my best friend.

11

Boom Town Bust Causes Health Care Crisis

1981 and early 1982 were boom times for the city of Houston. Our oil and chemical driven economies were fueled by $40.00 per barrel oil, up from the norm of $20.00-$25.00, and rapidly advancing exploration and development. Employment rates were so high that out of state license plates became a local joke, especially the "black-platers" from Michigan, where unemployment was frighteningly high.

Things turned around in Houston in late 1982 as worldwide petroleum over-development resulted in over-production and the market was flooded with cheap oil. The number of working oil rigs in Texas fell from around 4,500 to less than 2,000 by mid 1983. All of the related oil service and processing industries were affected and unemployment rose to over 16%. Many of these previously highly paid workers lost their benefits as well as their jobs, and more and more people were uninsured and unable to pay for medical care.

I had just been elected President of the Harris County Medical Society (the nation's fourth largest) having served the previous year as President Elect. It was customary for the president to lead the society in a "cause" during his presidency. Prior "causes" had included the development of emergency medical services, education on treatment of AIDS, accident prevention and other services to the public.

My "cause" was to develop a system to provide free care to the unemployed and uninsured, driven by local economics. At the first meeting of the executive board of the Harris County Medical Society in January of 1983, unanimous approval was expressed for my unique plan. The society membership would be asked to volunteer to provide free care to anyone who had lost their insurance due to the economic crisis. This care would not only be free, but would carry no obligation to pay at a later date. Response to the plan was heartening and over 1,000 members agreed to participate. Joining in our plan were several clinical laboratories and radiology groups. In addition, over 300 pharmacies agreed to fill prescriptions at their actual cost if the physician requested it. Several hospitals also agreed to provide free care including in-patient care to patients of physicians already on their staffs.

To administer the plan fairly and distribute the patients evenly and as efficiently as possible, a computer program was designed listing doctors by specialty and by zip code. Callers to the medical society office could then be quickly matched to an appropriate physician located near them.

It was critical that all the groundwork be in place before announcing this plan to the public, otherwise we feared chaos. Reporters from the newspaper and television found out about our program during the final week of preparation but agreed not to report it until the following Sunday. It was front page news on our leading paper that Sunday morning and the lead story on the local television news stations that day.

On Monday the major national networks all had reporters in Houston interviewing me and other Medical Society members, and watching and reporting the response to the plan. The first month over 5,500 calls were received with over 40% of callers seen by private volunteer physicians. To aid the Medical Society staff, the Auxiliary provided volunteers to receive calls and make referrals. Calls were coming in at the rate of 100 per day. A potential health care crisis was markedly lessened.

The day after the program was launched, an assistant to President Ronald Reagan called my office to extend an invitation to the White House for me and other leaders of the Society and Auxiliary. We were hosted in a special ceremony in the Roosevelt Room of the White House by President Reagan, Vice President George H. W. Bush and Secretary of Health and Human Services, Margaret Heckler.

I was asked to make a short speech to the President. I asked how long his speech was to be and was told it would be about five minutes. I replied that mine would be about three minutes. I then asked if the invitation included Jeanne. The

White House responded that the reception would be in the Roosevelt Room which is fairly small, and they were not sure Jeanne was included. I told them that I understood but if there should be enough room Jeanne would like to attend as she still had a "cauliflower ear" from working in the phone bank for President Reagan's election. They immediately replied, "Bring Mrs. Reed."

It was a great thrill to walk up to the guard house at the gate of the White House and announce that I had an appointment with the President. The guard asked my social security number, typed it into his computer, looked at the screen and at my face, placed a badge on my coat, and then sent me on to the door. A Marine guard opened the door; a butler took our coats and accompanied us into the room.

In just a few minutes President Reagan, Vice President Bush and Secretary Heckler came in. After introductions, I stood beside President Reagan at the podium and began my speech. I thought I had it memorized but began to feel uneasy and reached in my pocket for my notes. I apologized for using notes saying that I felt nervous but he immediately held up his notes and said "What do you think I have these for?" He put me right at ease.

After the exchange of speeches, the President and Vice President remained and talked with us for 15 minutes; something President Reagan's assistant said was unusual as he usually returned immediately to his office. We talked about the fact that Nancy Reagan's father, Dr. Loyal Davis, a neurosurgeon, had been my chief of surgery at Northwestern and that Jeanne had scrubbed for him when she was a student nurse. Apparently we had been well screened as he already knew those facts.

The American Medical Association held a reception for us at their Washington headquarters and I was able to spend about an hour with Secretary Heckler and tell her of my ideas for improving Medicare.

Many societies around the country considered similar plans for their communities. The Harris County Medical Society received accolades from many sources including the State Senate which passed a resolution honoring me and my fellow Harris county physicians. The Governor presented a certificate of recognition to me as president of the society.

The resilient Houston economy recovered slowly over several months, and calls for free care became more infrequent. The crisis had been averted, a testimonial to the physicians of Harris County.

12

God and Faith

Do you believe in God? If your answer is yes, what image comes to your mind as you consider who God is? Is it an artist's image like the one painted by Michelangelo on the ceiling of the Sistine Chapel? Or is it word pictures like those expressed in the Old or New Testaments of the Bible? Is it fair to envision God as someone made in our image since the Bible says that we are made in His image?

If you answered no, then I ask the same question. What image comes to your mind when you hear the name God? Is it the image you reject, or do you simply reject entirely the idea of a creator? If I had used the term "creative force" or "cosmic force" instead of the name God or Creator would your answer have changed? These are not simple or superficial questions but questions deserving an open mind and deep thought. I, too, have dealt with the problem of trying to comprehend the incomprehensible and have struggled to find my own words or mental picture of God the Creator.

When Jeanne and I first began to think about writing a family history, we looked at our reasons for doing it. Our thoughts quickly focused upon the succeeding generations. We wanted to pass along to them some understanding of their heritage. I jokingly called it giving them the ability to discover where all these crazy genes came from. We had done some genealogy research but mostly had a list of names of people to whom we are related but knew little or nothing about. We didn't want our names to be just two more on a list of relations. To Jeanne and me, the thing we wanted most to communicate was who we were, what made us tick—and nothing comes closer to describing that than the beliefs and faith that have guided our lives.

These are the things we want most for our progeny to understand because they have been the driving force in our wonderful and happy lives. These were the guiding principles of our life, or if you prefer, the rudder of our ship of state, or the guidance systems of our rocket. We felt that these precepts were of such great value to us that we wished to share them with our future generations.

Where did our faith come from? So many things played a part, but as we look back, the underlying principles by which we tried to live came not only from our families and religious training but from our education and life experiences as well. As I have mentioned previously, Jeanne's background was strictly conservative Missouri Synod Lutheran; mine was the rather liberal

Christian denomination of Disciples of Christ. Despite our differences in church background, Jeanne and I shared the same belief that Jesus was our Savior, and that he showed us in his life how to live with love as one's guiding principle.

This was the whole of Jeanne's very existence. I don't believe she ever went through a period of doubt or questioning of her faith. If she did, she never shared that with me. But I did. In my teen years, I not only doubted, but for a time, actually rejected much of what had been taught to me about religion. My college roommate's mother confided to me years later that she was convinced I was an atheist because I questioned so much.

As a child, I believed in a place somewhere above the clouds called heaven filled with "good" people and a place deep in the earth full of fire and "bad" people. Heaven had golden streets and pearly gates guarded by St. Peter himself. I can't remember specifically being taught these things but they were rather commonly-held beliefs, at least by children, in those days. When I saw Michelangelo's painting with the hand of God reaching out from the clouds and touching Adam this furthered the image of God as human-like and living in the clouds, watching us and guiding our lives.

None of this seemed to fit, however, with the scientific discoveries I was learning about in school, such as the age of the earth and its inhabitants as established by such irrefutable evidence as archeological digs and carbon dating. The 15.5 billion years estimated by these and other scientific measurements were widely divergent from the 4000 or so years deduced from the Bible. The universe and its continuing change and expansion confirmed by observation from the Hubbell telescope (the big bang) did not conform to placement of the earth, sun and stars as declared in the Bible.

Despite the fact that the Pope Clement VII accepted Copernicus' discovery that the earth and the planets revolved around the sun, many theologians considered the theory faulty and Martin Luther, a contemporary of Copernicus, called him a fool. Darwin proposed the theory of evolution of the species due to adaptation and survival of the fittest. This opposed the creation of each species and Darwin's theory, though controversial, was widely accepted, seeming to reinforce his conclusions.

No wonder my mind was confused. Six days? Impossible! Or were these cosmic days rather than earth days? It seemed that the more I questioned, the more confused I became. But I was clearly in a scientific mode and found it easier to question or reject the biblical truths in favor of scientific facts. I guess that was the period in my life when I thought I had the answer to everything or if not me, then science did.

But as I thought more deeply my mind gradually changed. Science and religion were not in conflict at all. Science was merely gaining a deeper insight as to the process of creation, not denying that creation occurred. In fact, the observations from the Hubbell telescope, proving beyond doubt that the universe is still expanding, evidenced conclusively that there was indeed a beginning, a time when all was created.

The term "creator" is a stumbling block to many and the term "God" an even greater stumbling block. But call it or him whatever you like, you simply cannot deny his existence. If our universe is expanding, then from what starting point and by what means? I think my mental process was developing as in the following joke: A conversation ensued between God and the scientist who had proclaimed that we no longer needed to believe in a creator God because he could create DNA in his own laboratory. God replied, "Show me."

The scientist began lining up the chemicals which he would use to produce the DNA when God spoke up. "Wait a minute," he said to the scientist. "Get your own chemicals."

As simple as this joke is, it should make one think more deeply. How *were* these basic elements formed? Were they created and collected in one spot and then propelled by a great force (the big bang) to the ends of the universe, or was matter formed by the energy created by the force itself? The relationship between energy and mass was proven by Albert Einstein with his formula $E=mc^2$, and particles of matter have been formed from energy, but an entire universe?

The very fact that we humans exist proves beyond any doubt that there was a starting point or beginning. Certainly the entire universe and all that is in it was created. It wasn't just there waiting to happen. I can't even imagine the power or force that was required to disperse all the matter of the universe a distance of 15.4 billion light years, the distance calculated from observations from the Hubbell telescope and still expanding.

The biggest man-made "bang" I know anything about was the atomic bomb blast at Hiroshima in World War II. Jeanne and I were able to visit the site which is now a park. The building at ground zero is still standing because the bomb was directly overhead and the building had a dome shaped roof which deflected the force. There was total destruction for a radius of about a mile and severe damage for another three miles. Not even a pock mark remains. We thought this was a huge force but it can't begin to compare to the original creative force, the "big bang."

How were the basic elements of matter created, and from what? How was light created? It is both a particle and a wave. It travels at a speed of 186,282 miles per second, a distance my mind can't really comprehend. But, even more mind-boggling, distances in our universe are calculated in light *years*. You must multiply the number of seconds in a year, 31,556,925, times the speed in miles per second, 186,282, to get the distance of just one light year. The nearest star to our sun is 4.3 light years away. Now you can do the math, I can do the math, but that distance is just too far for me to comprehend, other than a huge number on the paper.

What about life itself? Many scientists will say that as the earth was forming and when just the right conditions existed, the organic and inorganic elements and compounds which made up the earth in the presence of water (perhaps given energy from a lightning strike) combined to form simple proteins. These proteins then combined to form more complex chemicals from which emerged the first forms of life. Some believe that viruses were the first life forms because they are capable of reproducing, but the virus cannot reproduce unless it is in a living cell which provides its nourishment.

Therefore the first life must have been a simple one celled bacterium. Did I say simple? Just study how complex the simplest cell is with cell membrane, cytoplasm, organelles, hyper structures and more. This is not the sort of thing which will just develop because chemicals happen to be near each other and organize themselves. Can you even guess what the odds must be against the exact concentration of all the chemicals needed to form a protein being present in this solution or in mud? It has been said that the odds of this happening by chance are about as likely as a 747 aircraft being assembled by a tornado passing over a junkyard!

Yet these same scientists who insist upon applying the "scientific method" of observation, question, hypothesis, and experiment before conclusions are reached will accept the theory that all creation happened by chance. They do this with absolutely no evidence and in the face of staggering odds *against* such an arrangement. They theorize, with no confirming substantiation at all, that life began when certain chemicals came together solely by chance in a primordial soup or mud pond.

When I look around at the wonders of our world and look to the sky and see the wonders of our universe it is overwhelming. Chance? And when I look at the human body with all its complexities, I am just as overwhelmed. Chance? But even more so is the wonder of the human soul. It is far more than just consciousness or awareness. There is a divine, everlasting and indestructible quality to it which is what makes each of us so unique. The soul is, perhaps, the key to our own truly unique self. It is this characteristic which brings us closest to God.

And what is the most important element of our character or soul? I believe it is love. The closest I can come to an understanding of whom or what God is was expressed by the Apostle John who said "God is love". (1 John 4:8) Surely Jesus, God incarnate, was pure love. All his decisions and actions were based upon love. Wasn't the creation of the universe, the stars and planets and life itself an act of love? Scientists have developed robots that can do almost anything a human can do, often even better. But they cannot come close to developing a soul.

There was a time when I felt any of the questions I still had would ultimately be answered by scientific discovery and that only a dummy would still believe in a creator God. Surely men of great scientific knowledge would reject the idea of a creator. Wrong. I did a computer search of great scientists, thinkers, writers, philosophers and found that almost everyone I had heard of and hundreds more believed earnestly in God. Knowledge and science did not lead them away from belief, but instead reinforced their faith in a creator. The problem comes in trying to describe or visualize a being of such great power and intelligence, able to create such wonders. Now, with all our scientific knowledge, one must be a "dummy" to not believe in a creator.

No wonder we have difficulty comprehending a creator of such wonders. These things are beyond my grasp and I believe beyond the comprehension of any human being in the world. The human mind cannot appreciate fully these things, much less describe them in words or picture them in art. I think I understand better since a college classmate of mine, Rev. Richard B. Schellhase, characterized our dilemma as a "language box" or a "language prison" and pointed out that language itself is a symbolic system, not reality itself—nor can it properly describe reality. In trying to describe such a Creator we must use human terms that we can grasp, but we must accept the fact that any description is going to fall far short of the actual. But it is obvious that we do exist. Just look in the mirror and pinch yourself. We are surrounded by wonders that are beyond our full intellectual capacity. There had to be a beginning, a creation and therefore a creator.

To me, faith means knowing for sure that the creator is real even though I cannot fully understand. If I exist then He must exist. I delight when someone asks if I believe in God. My answer is that I believe with my whole heart and mind but don't ask me to tell you who God is. I only know that He is the beginning, the creator. I can only use terms that I do comprehend, knowing full well that God is far, far more complex and well beyond my ability to characterize in words.

It should be obvious by now that I remain confused and am still full of doubts. But these doubts are no longer about the existence of God but about His true nature. I know this is something I will not understand until I am face to face with

Him and in the meantime I am content to use the name God to refer to Him, and to address Him as Father despite the fact that these human terms fall far short of the reality.

I remain thankful for the revelation He gave us through the life, death and resurrection of His son, Jesus. The apostles proudly and boldly proclaimed what they had seen in the face of hostility which led to their own deaths. The apostle John said "God is love" and Jesus showed us how a human being can live a life of love. He also said "Know me and you know the father." I feel that love is the image of God in which we have been created. Both Jeanne and I have believed profoundly in the creator God whose Son showed us the way to live life. What a wonderful world it would be if we could really live a life of love following His example.

Please just read on to see the great scientists of the world who were able to reason beyond the prejudices of their time and to believe intelligently and rationally in God. Faith is no longer nebulous; it is based upon solid evidence.

Famous Scientists Who Believed in God
Belief in God

Is belief in the existence of God irrational? These days, many famous scientists are also strong proponents of atheism. However, in the past and even today, many scientists believe that God exists and is responsible for what we see in nature. This is a small sampling of scientists who contributed to the development of modern science while believing in God. Although many people believe in a "God of the gaps", these scientists, and still others alive today, believe because of the evidence.

Rich Deem

1. **Nicholas Copernicus (1473-1543)**
   Copernicus was the Polish astronomer who put forward the first mathematically based system of planets going around the sun. He attended various European universities, and became a Canon in the Catholic Church in 1497. His new system was actually first presented in the Vatican gardens in 1533 before Pope Clement VII who approved, and urged Copernicus to publish it around this time. Copernicus was never under any threat of religious persecution - and was urged to publish both by Catholic Bishop Guise, Cardinal Schonberg, and the Protestant Professor George Rheticus. Copernicus referred sometimes to God in his works, and did not see his system as in conflict with the Bible.
2. **Sir Francis Bacon (1561-1627)**
   Bacon was a philosopher who is known for establishing the scientific method of inquiry based on experimentation and inductive reasoning. In *De Interpretatione Naturae Prooemium*, Bacon established his goals as being the discovery of truth, service to his country, and service to the

church. Although his work was based upon experimentation and reasoning, he rejected atheism as being the result of insufficient depth of philosophy, stating, "It is true, that a little philosophy inclineth man's mind to atheism, but depth in philosophy bringeth men's minds about to religion; for while the mind of man looketh upon second causes scattered, it may sometimes rest in them, and go no further; but when it beholdeth the chain of them confederate, and linked together, it must needs fly to Providence and Deity." (*Of Atheism*)

3. **Johannes Kepler (1571-1630)**
Kepler was a brilliant mathematician and astronomer. He did early work on light, and established the laws of planetary motion about the sun. He also came close to reaching the Newtonian concept of universal gravity - well before Newton was born! His introduction of the idea of force in astronomy changed it radically in a modern direction. Kepler was an extremely sincere and pious Lutheran, whose works on astronomy contain writings about how space and the heavenly bodies represent the Trinity. Kepler suffered no persecution for his open avowal of the sun-centered system, and, indeed, was allowed as a Protestant to stay in Catholic Graz as a Professor (1595-1600) when other Protestants had been expelled!

4. **Galileo Galilei (1564-1642)**
   Galileo is often remembered for his conflict with the Roman Catholic Church. His controversial work on the solar system was published in 1633. It had no proofs of a sun-centered system (Galileo's telescope discoveries did not indicate a moving earth) and his one "proof" based upon the tides was invalid. It ignored the correct elliptical orbits of planets published twenty five years earlier by Kepler. Since his work finished by putting the Pope's favorite argument in the mouth of the simpleton in the dialogue, the Pope (an old friend of Galileo's) was very offended. After the "trial" and being forbidden to teach the sun-centered system, Galileo did his most useful theoretical work, which was on dynamics. Galileo expressly said that the Bible cannot err, and saw his system as an alternate interpretation of the biblical texts.

5. **Rene Descartes (1596-1650)**
   Descartes was a French mathematician, scientist and philosopher who has been called the father of modern philosophy. His school studies made him dissatisfied with previous philosophy: He had a deep religious faith as a Roman Catholic, which he retained to his dying day, along with a resolute, passionate desire to discover the truth. At the age of 24 he had a dream, and felt the vocational call to seek to bring knowledge together in one system of thought. His system began by asking what

could be known if all else were doubted - suggesting the famous "I think therefore I am". Actually, it is often forgotten that the next step for Descartes was to establish the near certainty of the existence of God - for only if God both exists and would not want us to be deceived by our experiences - can we trust our senses and logical thought processes. God is, therefore, central to his whole philosophy. What he really wanted to see was that his philosophy be adopted as standard Roman Catholic teaching. Rene Descartes and Francis Bacon (1561-1626) are generally regarded as the key figures in the development of scientific methodology. Both had systems in which God was important, and both seem more devout than the average for their era.

6. **Isaac Newton (1642-1727)**

   In optics, mechanics, and mathematics, Newton was a figure of undisputed genius and innovation. In all his science (including chemistry) he saw mathematics and numbers as central. What is less well known is that he was devoutly religious and saw numbers as involved in understanding God's plan for history from the Bible. He did a considerable work on biblical numerology, and, though aspects of his beliefs were not orthodox, he thought theology was very important. In his system of physics, God is essential to the nature and absoluteness of space. In *Principia* he stated, "The most beautiful system of the sun, planets, and comets, could only proceed from the counsel and dominion on an intelligent and powerful Being."

7. **Robert Boyle (1791-1867)**
One of the founders and key early members of the Royal Society, Boyle gave his name to "Boyle's Law" for gases, and also wrote an important work on chemistry. *Encyclopedia Britannica* says of him: "By his will he endowed a series of Boyle lectures, or sermons, which still continue, 'for proving the Christian religion against notorious infidels . . . ' As a devout Protestant, Boyle took a special interest in promoting the Christian religion abroad, giving money to translate and publish the New Testament into Irish and Turkish. In 1690 he developed his theological views in *The Christian Virtuoso*, which he wrote to show that the study of nature was a central religious duty." Boyle wrote against atheists in his day (the notion that atheism is a modern invention is a myth), and was clearly much more devoutly Christian than the average in his era.

8. **Michael Faraday (1791-1867)**
Michael Faraday was the son of a blacksmith who became one of the greatest scientists of the 19th century. His work on electricity and magnetism not only revolutionized physics, but led to much of our lifestyles today, which depends on them (including computers and telephone lines and, so, web sites). Faraday was a devoutly Christian member of the Sandemanians, which significantly influenced him and strongly

affected the way in which he approached and interpreted nature. Originating from Presbyterians, the Sandemanians rejected the idea of state churches, and tried to go back to a New Testament type of Christianity.

9. **Gregor Mendel (1822-1884)**

   Mendel was the first to lay the mathematical foundations of genetics, in what came to be called "Mendelianism". He began his research in 1856 (three years before Darwin published his *Origin of Species*) in the garden of the Monastery in which he was a monk. Mendel was elected Abbot of his Monastery in 1868. His work remained comparatively unknown until the turn of the century, when a new generation of botanists began finding similar results and "rediscovered" him (though their ideas were not identical to his). An interesting point is that the 1860's was notable for formation of the X-Club, which was dedicated to lessening religious influences and propagating an image of "conflict" between science and religion. One sympathizer was Darwin's cousin Francis Galton, whose scientific interest was in genetics (a proponent of eugenics - selective breeding among humans to "improve" the stock). He was writing how the "priestly mind" was not conducive to science while, at around the same time, an Austrian monk was making the breakthrough in genetics. The rediscovery of the work of Mendel came too late to affect Galton's contribution.

10. **William Thomson Kelvin (1824-1907)**
Kelvin was foremost among the small group of British scientists who helped to lay the foundations of modern physics. His work covered many areas of physics, and he was said to have more letters after his name than anyone else in the Commonwealth, since he received numerous honorary degrees from European Universities, which recognized the value of his work. He was a very committed Christian, who was certainly more religious than the average for his era. Interestingly, his fellow physicists George Gabriel Stokes (1819-1903) and James Clerk Maxwell (1831-1879) were also men of deep Christian commitment, in an era when many were nominal, apathetic, or anti-Christian. The Encyclopedia Britannica says "Maxwell is regarded by most modern physicists as the scientist of the 19th century who had the greatest influence on 20th century physics; he is ranked with Sir Isaac Newton and Albert Einstein for the fundamental nature of his contributions." Lord Kelvin was an Old Earth creationist, who estimated the Earth's age to be somewhere between 20 million and 100 million years, with an upper limit at 500 million years based on cooling rates (a low estimate due to his lack of knowledge about radiogenic heating).

11. **Max Planck (1858-1947)**
Planck made many contributions to physics, but is best known for quantum theory, which revolutionized our understanding of the atomic and sub-atomic worlds.

In his 1937 lecture "Religion and Naturwissenschaft," Planck expressed the view that God is everywhere present, and held that "the holiness of the unintelligible Godhead is conveyed by the holiness of symbols." Atheists, he thought, attach too much importance to what are merely symbols. Planck was a churchwarden from 1920 until his death, and believed in an almighty, all-knowing, beneficent God (though not necessarily a personal one). Both science and religion wage a "tireless battle against skepticism and dogmatism, against unbelief and superstition" with the goal "toward God!"

12. **Albert Einstein (1879-1955)**

Einstein is probably the best known and most highly revered scientist of the twentieth century, and is associated with major revolutions in our thinking about time, gravity, and the conversion of matter to energy ($E=mc^2$). Although <u>never coming to belief in a personal God</u>, he recognized the impossibility of a non-created universe. The *Encyclopedia Britannica* says of him: "Firmly denying atheism, Einstein expressed a belief in "Spinoza's God who reveals himself in the harmony of what exists." This actually motivated his interest in science, as he once remarked to a young physicist: "I want to know how God created this world, I am not interested in this or that phenomenon, in the spectrum of this or that element. I want to know His thoughts, the rest are details." Einstein's famous epithet on the "uncertainty principle" was "God does not play dice" - and to him this was a real statement about a God in whom he believed. A famous saying of his was "Science without religion is lame, religion without science is blind."

50 Nobel Laureates and Other Great Scientists Who Believe in God

Tihomir Dimitrov's online book of quotations *50 Nobel Laureates and Other Great Scientists Who Believe in God* (2007) is mostly about scientists, although it also features sections about non-scientist Nobel Prize winners. The book can be found at http://nobelists.net/ Everyone should read this great book, especially if you feel that you are an agnostic or an atheist.

The author's website describes the book: "This book is an anthology of well-documented quotations. It is a free e-book." This portion is printed with the author's permission.

It should be noted that *50 Nobel Laureates* is written primarily for inspirational purposes and is not intended to be a source of detailed or balanced biographical data. Nevertheless, the book is a treasure trove of interesting information. Also note that the author's criteria for including Nobel Laureates who "believe in God" does not imply a specific type of belief or adherence to any specific religious group or denomination. The individuals included in the book represent a wide range of religious beliefs, religious affiliation, and religious practice.

50 Nobel Laureates includes chapters on the following individuals:

PART I. Nobel Scientists (20-21 Century)		
Albert Einstein	Nobel Laureate in Physics	Jewish
Max Planck	Nobel Laureate in Physics	Protestant
Erwin Schrodinger	Nobel Laureate in Physics	Catholic
Werner Heisenberg	Nobel Laureate in Physics	Lutheran
Robert Millikan	Nobel Laureate in Physics	probably Congregationalist
Charles Hard Townes	Nobel Laureate in Physics	United Church of Christ (raised Baptist)
Arthur Schawlow	Nobel Laureate in Physics	Methodist
William D. Phillips	Nobel Laureate in Physics	Methodist
William H. Bragg	Nobel Laureate in Physics	Anglican
Guglielmo Marconi	Nobel Laureate in Physics	Catholic and Anglican
Arthur Compton	Nobel Laureate in Physics	Presbyterian
Arno Penzias	Nobel Laureate in Physics	Jewish
Nevill Mott	Nobel Laureate in Physics	Anglican
Isidor Isaac Rabi	Nobel Laureate in Physics	Jewish
Abdus Salam	Nobel Laureate in Physics	Muslim
Antony Hewish	Nobel Laureate in Physics	Christian (denomination?)
Joseph H. Taylor, Jr.	Nobel Laureate in Physics	Quaker
Alexis Carrel	Nobel Laureate in Medicine and Physiology	Catholic

John Eccles	Nobel Laureate in Medicine and Physiology	Catholic
Joseph Murray	Nobel Laureate in Medicine and Physiology	Catholic
Ernst Chain	Nobel Laureate in Medicine and Physiology	Jewish
George Wald	Nobel Laureate in Medicine and Physiology	Jewish
Ronald Ross	Nobel Laureate in Medicine and Physiology	Christian (denomination?)
Derek Barton	Nobel Laureate in Chemistry	Christian (denomination?)
Christian Anfinsen	Nobel Laureate in Chemistry	Jewish
Walter Kohn	Nobel Laureate in Chemistry	Jewish
Richard Smalley	Nobel Laureate in Chemistry	Christian (denomination?)
PART II. Nobel Writers (20-21 Century)		
T.S. Eliot	Nobel Laureate in Literature	Anglo-Catholic (Anglican)
Rudyard Kipling	Nobel Laureate in Literature	Anglican
Alexander Solzhenitsyn	Nobel Laureate in Literature	Russian Orthodox
François Mauriac	Nobel Laureate in Literature	Catholic
Hermann Hesse	Nobel Laureate in Literature	Christian; Buddhist?
Winston Churchill	Nobel Laureate in Literature	Anglican
Jean-Paul Sartre	Nobel Laureate in Literature	Lutheran; Freudian; Marxist; atheist; Messianic Jew

Sigrid Undset	Nobel Laureate in Literature	Catholic (previously Lutheran)
Rabindranath Tagore	Nobel Laureate in Literature	Hindu
Rudolf Eucken	Nobel Laureate in Literature	Christian (denomination?)
Isaac Singer	Nobel Laureate in Literature	Jewish
PART III. Nobel Peace Laureates (20-21 Century)		
Albert Schweitzer	Nobel Peace Prize Laureate	Lutheran
Jimmy Carter	Nobel Peace Prize Laureate	Baptist (former Southern Baptist)
Theodore Roosevelt	Nobel Peace Prize Laureate	Dutch Reformed; Episcopalian
Woodrow Wilson	Nobel Peace Prize Laureate	Presbyterian
Frederik de Klerk	Nobel Peace Prize Laureate	Dutch Reformed
Nelson Mandela	Nobel Peace Prize Laureate	Christian (denomination?)
Kim Dae-Jung	Nobel Peace Prize Laureate	Catholic
Dag Hammarskjold	Nobel Peace Prize Laureate	Christian (denomination?)
Martin Luther King, Jr.	Nobel Peace Prize Laureate	Baptist
Adolfo Perez Esquivel	Nobel Peace Prize Laureate	Catholic
Desmond Tutu	Nobel Peace Prize Laureate	Anglican
John R. Mott	Nobel Peace Prize Laureate	Methodist
Part IV. Founders of Modern Science (16-21 Century)		
Isaac Newton	Founder of Classical Physics and Infinitesimal Calculus	Anglican (rejected Trinitarianism, i.e., Athanasianism; believed in the Arianism of the Primitive Church)

Galileo Galilei	Founder of Experimental Physics	Catholic
Nicolaus Copernicus	Founder of Heliocentric Cosmology	Catholic (priest)
Johannes Kepler	Founder of Physical Astronomy and Modern Optics	Lutheran
Francis Bacon	Founder of the Scientific Inductive Method	Anglican
René Descartes	Founder of Analytical Geometry and Modern Philosophy	Catholic
Blaise Pascal	Founder of Hydrostatics, Hydrodynamics, and the Theory of Probabilities	Jansenist
Michael Faraday	Founder of Electronics and Electro-Magnetics	Sandemanian
James Clerk Maxwell	Founder of Statistical Thermodynamics	Presbyterian; Anglican; Baptist
Lord Kelvin	Founder of Thermodynamics and Energetics	Anglican
Robert Boyle	Founder of Modern Chemistry	Anglican
William Harvey	Founder of Modern Medicine	Anglican (nominal)
John Ray	Founder of Modern Biology and Natural History	Calvinist (denomination?)

Gottfried Wilhelm Leibniz	German Mathematician and Philosopher, Founder of Infinitesimal Calculus	Lutheran
Charles Darwin	Founder of the Theory of Evolution	Anglican (nominal); Unitarian
Ernst Haeckel	German Biologist, the Most Influential Evolutionist in Continental Europe	
Thomas H. Huxley	English Biologist and Evolutionist, Famous As "Darwin's Bulldog"	
Joseph J. Thomson	Nobel Laureate in Physics, Discoverer of the Electron, Founder of Atomic Physics	Anglican
Louis Pasteur	Founder of Microbiology and Immunology	Catholic
Part V. Great Philosophers (17-21 Century)		
Immanuel Kant	One of the Greatest Philosophers in the History of Western Philosophy	Lutheran
Jean-Jacques Rousseau	Founder of Modern Deism	born Protestant; converted as a teen to Catholic

Voltaire	French Philosopher and Historian, One of the Most Influential Thinkers of the Enlightenment	raised in Jansenism
David Hume	Scottish Empiricist Philosopher, Historian, and Economist, Founder of Modern Skepticism	Church of Scotland (Presbyterian)
Spinoza	Dutch-Jewish Philosopher, the Chief Exponent of Modern Rationalism	Judaism; later pantheism/deism
Giordano Bruno	Italian Philosopher, Astronomer, and Mathematician, Founder of the Theory of the Infinite Universe	Catholic
George Berkeley	Irish Philosopher and Mathematician, Founder of Modern Idealism, Famous as "The Precursor of Mach and Einstein"	Anglican
John Stuart Mill	English Philosopher and Economist, the Major Exponent of Utilitarianism	agnostic; Utilitarian

Richard Swinburne	Oxford Professor of Philosophy, One of the Most Influential Theistic Philosophers	

PART VI. Other Religious Nobelists

60 more Nobel Prize winners are listed (32 scientists, 17 writers, 11 Nobel Nobel Peace Laureates)

PART VII. Nobelists, Philosophers, and Scientists on Jesus

Quotes by 16 individuals about their beliefs about Jesus
- Alexis Carrel
- Albert Einstein
- Arthur Compton
- Robert Millikan
- Francois Mauriac
- Sigrid Undset
- T.S. Eliot
- Mother Theresa
- Albert Schweitzer
- Theodore Roosevelt
- Frederik de Klerk
- John R. Mott
- Kim Dae-Jung
- Martin Luther King, Jr.
- Jimmy Carter
- Blaise Pascal

Some Famous Scientists who were Christians

John Philoponus	late 6th Century	Aristotle's early Christian critic
Hugh of St. Victor	1096-1141	theologian of science
Robert Grosseteste	1168-1253	reform-minded bishop-scientist
Roger Bacon	1220-1292	Doctor Mirabiles
Dietrich von Frieberg	1250-1310	the priest who solved the mystery of the rainbow
Thomas Bradwardine	1290-1349	student of motion
Nicole Oresme	1320-1382	inventor of scientific graphic techniques
Nicholas of Cusa	1401-1464	grappler with infinity
Georgias Agricola	1495-1555	founder of metallurgy
Johannes Kepler	1571-1630	discoverer of the laws of planetary motion
Johannes Baptista van Helmont	1579-1644	founder of pneumatic chemistry and chemical physiology

Francesco Maria Grimaldi	1618-1663	discoverer of the diffraction of light	Catholic
Blaise Pascal	1623-1662	mathematical prodigy and universal genius	
Robert Boyle	1627-1691	founder of modern chemistry	
John Ray	1627-1705	cataloger of British flora and fauna	Calvinist
Isaac Barrow	1630-1677	Newton's teacher	
Antonie van Leeuwenhoek	1632-1723	discoverer of bacteria	
Niels Seno	1638-1686	founder of geology	
James Bradley	1693-1762	discoverer of the aberration of starlight	
Ewald Georg von Kleist	1700-1748	inventor of the Leyden jar	
Carolus Linnaeus	1707-1778	classifer of all living things	
Leonhard Euler	1707-1783	the prolific mathematician	
John Dalton	1766-1844	founder of modern atomic theory	

Thomas Young	1773-1829	first to conduct a double-slit experiment with light	
David Brewster	1781-1868	researcher of polarized light	
William Buckland	1784-1856	geologist of the Noahic flood	
Adem Sedgwick	1785-1873	geologist of the Cambrian	
Augustin-Jean Fresnel	1788-1827	the physicist of light waves	
Augustin Louis Cauchy	1789-1857	soulwinning mathematician	
Michael Faraday	1791-1867	giant of electrical research	
John Frederick William Herschel	1792-1871	cataloger of the Southern skies	
Matthew Fontaine Maury	1806-1873	pathfinder of the seas	
Philip Henry Gosse	1810-1888	popular naturalist	
Asa Gray	1810-1888	influential botanist	
James Dwight Dana	1813-1895	systematizer of minerology	

George Boole	1815-1864	discoverer of pure mathematics	
James Prescott Joule	1818-1889	originator of Joule's Law	
John Couch Adams	1819-1892	Co-discoverer of Neptune	
George Gabriel Stokes	1819-1903	theorist of fluorescence	
Gregor Mendel	1822-1884	pioneer in genetics	
William Thomson, Lord Kelvin	1824-1907	physicist of thermodynamics	
Georg Friedrich Bernhard Riemann	1829-1907	the non-Euclidean geometer behind relativity theory	
James Clerk Maxwell	1831-1879	father of modern physics	
Edward William Morley	1838-1923	Michelson's partner in measuring the speed of light	
Pierre-Maurice-Marie Duhem	1861-1923	the physicist who recovered the science of the Middle Ages	
Georges Lemaitre	1894-1966	the priest who showed us the universe is expanding	

| George Washington Carver | 1864-1943 | pioneer in chemurgy | |
| Arthur Stanley Eddington | 1882-1944 | the astronomer who ruled stellar theory | |

Reprinted with permission from Tihomir Dimitrov

Is that not an impressive list? Now who is the dummy? Which list would you like your name to be on?

13

Parenting

My children asked that I include a chapter on parenting. How I wish they had asked while Jeanne was still alive! She was our parenting expert. She always, I hope jokingly, said that she had six children (Me being the sixth). I'm certain the children asked for this chapter because they felt that they had been well parented. If results are the measure, then certainly they were. You would have to search far and wide to find such a wonderful group of adults as these five children grew up to be. We are extremely proud of each one of them.

Jeanne and I both claimed that all we knew about parenting we learned from our children. Certainly this was true of me, but Jeanne seemed to have a special knack all her own. First, she possessed an infinite supply of patience, something everyone who knew her commented upon. It is certainly one of the most important attributes for successful parenting.

There are, of course, many things about parenting that can be taught in a class and there is an advantage to knowing them before the first baby is born. I refer to such things as breast feeding, proper foods and at what age to introduce them, immunization schedules, and even such basics as how to change a diaper, how warm a formula should be, and proper bathing techniques. These things can be learned on the run and I am sure that they are not the things the children wanted me to write about. They know what is most important because they have lived it with their own children and all have proven themselves to be expert parents.

First, and beyond any doubt, the most important thing of all is that children are born into a loving home, a God-centered home. After all, "God is love." Those are the words of the apostle John who, I believe, was the one who most clearly understood the nature of God. Jesus demonstrated how to live a life of love. If the parents are devoted to each other and show and express their love for each other the child is immediately made to feel secure and is able to relate in the same manner. This kind of environment encourages love and respect for others.

Secondly, the child must know that they are loved and wanted. If you don't want children until a later time, use birth control. That goes for both sexes as there is no 100% effective method, but if both use birth control the odds of preventing pregnancy become very close to perfect. If you feel you never want children, get surgically fixed. Vasectomy for men is quick, simple, easy and almost pain free. Tubal ligation for women is a bit more complex, but still very easy. Both can be reversed with good success if you change your minds and really want children later.

Both parents need to not only show their love but to express it verbally over and over. It must be sincere. You can't fake it. If the pregnancy came at an inconvenient time because of job or personal problems or financial problems, those problems are yours, not the child's and they cannot be allowed to affect your relationship with the child.

Thirdly, the child or children must be more important to you than your own personal wants or needs. They must be able to command your attention and time over other considerations. You must talk to them at their level, play childish games with them, encourage them in their accomplishments, and take time from work to attend their activities. Set aside time for specific activities centered upon each child. Each child should feel their value to you. One thing that worked so well for us was to have a "date" or take a trip with each child alone. In this setting, there was no sibling rivalry and the child was the center of attention. It was a great bonding experience for both parent and child and every one of the children and grandchildren have said that it was a most meaningful experience to them.

Joel III's teen years were a challenge. He was so ready to act independently and I was so *un*ready to let go of my authority to make all his decisions for him. Thank God for Dr. Kennett, who convinced me that I was the problem and should back off. His best recommendation was for the two of us to take a trip together. That trip (to Europe) truly made me a better parent. In fact, everything

I know about parenting I learned from children, and now my grandchildren. The true treasures in life are those relationships.

Be there whenever your children need you and above all be patient. Remember that they are children and do not think and act as adults so do not expect them to. They reason like children, not like adults, and you must reach their level as they cannot reach yours. If something is important to them, it should be important to you.

Remember how much they are influenced by their peers. On the street and often in school, they are exposed to conduct which is the exact opposite of what you desire for them. Center their activities as much as possible with groups who think and act as you wish. What better example of that is there than the church? Christians are not perfect by any means—but at least as a group we all are striving for a virtuous life. Church sports leagues, youth activities clubs, bible studies—all these place the child in an environment which is far more likely to be virtuous than "street" groups or activities. Brownies, Boy Scouts and Girl Scouts are also excellent. Too much idle time is poison.

Finally, remember that children learn by what they see. What you tell them has only a fraction of the effect that your actions show. Do you think you can influence them to not use drugs if you smoke or drink? Remember that nicotine and alcohol are both drugs—legal, yes, but addictive nevertheless—and children seem to know this better than most adults. These legal drugs do more damage than most illegal drugs. If you want your children to avoid drugs, show them that you don't use them.

Yes, you must teach them honesty, integrity, personal responsibility, honor, respect, kindness and giving. But no matter how much you talk, it is your actions your children will see and copy. I think Edgar Guest said it best in his poem "Sermons We See":

Sermons We See
I'd rather see a sermon than hear one any day;
I'd rather one should walk with me than merely
    tell the way.
The eye's a better pupil and more willing than the
    ear,
Fine counsel is confusing, but example's always
    clear;
And the best of all preachers are the men who
    live their creeds,
For to see good put in action is what everybody
    needs.
I soon can learn to do it if you'll let me see it done;
I can watch your hands in action but your tongue
    too fast may run.
And the lecture you deliver may be very wise and
    true,
But I'd rather get my lessons by observing what
    you do;
For I might misunderstand you and the high
    advice you give,
But there's no misunderstanding how you act and
    how you live.
When I see a deed of kindness, I am eager to be
    kind.

When a weaker brother stumbles and a strong man stays behind
Just to see if he can help him, then the wish grows strong in me
To become as big and thoughtful as I know a friend to be.
And all travelers can witness that the best of guides today
Is not the one who tells them but the one who shows the way.
One good man teaches many, men believe what they behold;
One deed of kindness noticed is worth forty that are told.
Who stands with men of honor learns to hold his honor dear,
For right living speaks a language which to everyone is clear.
Though an able speaker charms me with his eloquence, I say,
I'd rather see a sermon that to hear one, any day.

The greatest strength in our parenting was the powerful love we had for each other and for each of our children. Even at times when we needed to discipline them, we always showed our love for them although sometimes it was "tough love." We both enjoyed being with them for the events in their lives whether it was a school event or sporting event, and cheered them on for their accomplishments. Jeanne and I learned early on that we could not ask the child whether an event or contest was a "big deal" or not. They would always answer that it was not, but believe me, any event or contest in which the child is a participant *is* a "big deal" to them. They cherish your attendance and your cheering them on more than you know. It may not be apparent at the time, but later, sometimes years later, you will know how much your simple presence enhanced their self worth and enriched their character.

Don't ever keep a troubled marriage together "for the kids." They will be miserable in that environment, just as you would be. Instead, get help from a competent marriage counselor, spiritual advisor, psychologist or psychiatrist and stick with it until the issues are solved. Divorce usually means just moving your problems elsewhere and can be devastating to all concerned, especially the children. Furthermore, the underlying problem just moves with you to affect future relationships. Children can be your greatest joy in life, but they can't do it alone. They need your love, attention, respect and guidance.

For our 50th anniversary, niece Jeanne Miller solicited answers to many questions from family members including the children and grandchildren. She then sorted the answers and made a calendar with a response on each day. It was a monumental work and has remained one of our greatest treasures. I still turn the page each day and many entries bring a tear. Also on that anniversary, Caryl collected panels for a quilt with each person designing a picture or placing a comment about their fondest memories to be put on their panel.

Then Linda Zucconi (Jennifer's mother-in-law) pieced them together into a beautiful quilt. I promise you that no parent can look at such a loving piece of art without tears of happiness filling their eyes. Perhaps the children's own comments will give more insight than I can into what aspects of parenting meant the most to them. It will make it clear as to what was important to them. I have selected a few from the many they wrote that relate to parenting. Their comments confirm what Jeanne and I believed: Good parenting cannot come from study of practices or techniques. It will only come as a result of parents' love and commitment to their children.

Remember, I said that all I know about parenting my children taught me? Well here's the proof in their own words.

> "The most important thing my parents taught me about life is always work hard and go the extra mile." *Joel III*
>
> "My parent's marriage is successful because they live each day thinking of the other person's needs." *Caryl*
>
> "I love Grandpa because he's always willing to take time away from what he is doing to talk or play with the grandkids." *Catherine*
>
> "One of my happiest memories of Dad were our "dates" together, they were so special." *Caryl*
>
> "The most important thing my parents taught me about life is: enjoy it, don't waste it, and make a difference." *Ann*
>
> "Jeanne and Joel were really there for me when....when have they not been there?" *Bill*

"Grandma taught me to have patience and it will pay off in the end." *Eric*

"My most moving memory of Mom is when she first held my children." *Ann*

"The thing I admire most about Joel is he still loves playing with the children, never tiring of them or the games they play. He really has a young spirit." *Lisa*

"I like to visit Grandma and Papa because they make such a big fuss over me." *Christian*

"The most important thing my parents taught me about marriage is that it is not a 50-50 partnership, but a partnership where 100% is given by each one." *Caryl*

"Grandpa taught me that Papas and Grandmas can fix ANYTHING." *Elyse*

"The most important things my parents taught me about being a parent were: hugs and cuddles every day, creating memories is more important than spending a lot of money on the children and the best gift I can give my children is myself." *Ann*

"Papa taught me not to lie. That was very important to me." *Caroline*

"I like to visit Grandma and Grandpa because they always seem to enjoy our company as much as we enjoy theirs. I feel so at home when I'm at their house." *Catherine*

"The thing I admire most about Mom is her patience. She keeps the family balanced." *Ann*

"Grandma taught me sincerity. Patience. Love. The list could go on and on. My Grandma is such a real person. In everything she does, you can see her true love for others. Never have

I heard her raise her voice in anger. Never have I heard her take credit for her kind actions, even when they are due. And I have never seen her put herself before another. I try every day to remember these qualities and make them more a part of who I am." *Jennifer*

"My most moving memory of Jeanne is one day, she said, "Can I just call you my daughter because you are so special and daughter-in-law just doesn't seem right anymore?" Of course, I said yes!" *Lisa*

"One of my happiest memories of Mom is her being able to be there at each of my kid's births." *Joel III*

"The one thing I admire most about Dad is the fact that he had one of the most demanding schedules of any I knew growing up. He balanced long days with everything that a large family did. In spite of everything, I never ever remember him missing being present at anything we kids were involved with at the time." *Caryl*

"I love Grandma because she loves me so much." *Bryan*

"The thing I admire most about Jeanne is her ability to remain calm and collected regardless of what is going on around her. I don't think I have ever seen her ruffled or bent out of shape because of the way something was going. Whatever happens, she takes it all in stride and keeps going. What a wonderful lady!" *Al*

"The one thing I admire about Mom is her patience and strength, and her ability to always see the good in situations where others tend to see the bad." *Caryl*

"Jeanne taught me the importance of being gracious, dignified and kind, and to love unconditionally. I'm still learning." *Laurel*

"Grandma makes me laugh when my parents won't let me do something and grandma thinks I can, so she convinces my parents to let me." *Ryan*

"One thing that really stands out on the "happiest" scale is seeing how Joel treats his grandchildren. There are 12 of them now and he gets a tremendous amount of joy seeing each one." *Rick*

"The best thing Jeanne and Joel did in raising my spouse was in instilling in her the value of God and family. This cannot be taught by lecture. It can only be learned by observation and living in that environment. When you look at the five children and their families, and the next generation as Jennifer and Tom begin their family, it appears as if these values have been passed on. There is no greater gift than love, devotion and respect for God and family." *Al*

"The one thing I admire most about Mom is her patience and her constant giving. She is always doing for others." *Mary*

"I love Grandma because she's loving and giving." *Alissa*

"The one thing I admire most about Jeanne is her selflessness. She lives through her unqualified giving to others." *George*

"The most important thing my parents taught me about life is whatever you do, be the best." *John*

"I remember once when I was sick with pneumonia. My chest hurt so bad. Dad came home from work at lunch and brought ice cream. When he hugged me, I remember all my hurt disappeared. To this day I can remember that special feeling." *Ann*

"The one thing I admire most about Mom is her ability to remain calm when all about her is chaos, and her ability to say the right thing to make you feel better when times are tough." *Joel III*

"Mom was really there for me when I needed a friend to talk to when Al's company closed his division. I felt so helpless. She helped me see that my faith was misplaced. It should be in Al and not the company that previously signed his checks, and, of course, that God had a plan in all of it. She was right, but she also felt my pain and my fear and was always there with an ear and a hug. She's my best friend." *Caryl*

"Mom was really there for me when Christian was born. She made me so many dinners so I didn't have to cook and was always taking Bryan and Elyse to and from school and various activities. I don't know how she and dad did it all. (But I can't limit it to this- she's always there for me)." *Mary*

"The greatest gift my parents gave me is unconditional love." *Ann*

"The one thing I admire most about Jeanne is her ability to bite her tongue when she must be dying to offer advice." *Laurel*

"My most moving memory of Jeanne and Joel would be hard to say since there are so many. It would have to be the way they take time to make all their children and grandchildren feel important and special." *Bill*

"I have so many fond memories of times spent with Grandma. Walking to Tamarac Park to slide on the slides and swing on the swings. Watching Jeopardy and trying to convince her to become a contestant. Going to the Woodlands pool to swim, eat hamburgers and chips for lunch. Many years of seeing the Nutcracker ballet together at Christmas. And some of my favorite times with Grandma were those that we just spent sitting and talking together." *Jennifer*

"I admire Jeanne's ability to love unconditionally. This has been one of the greatest lessons I've learned from her." *Laurel*

"I'll always treasure the way Auntie Jeanne made me extra special when she'd say "Honestly, that Georgia!" whenever I did something she thought was wonderful." *Georgia*

"The greatest gift my parents gave me was self-reliance." *John*

"My parents' marriage is successful because they always take time to be with each other. They make each other feel that the other is the most important person in their life, which they are. I remember Dad coming home each day from work and giving Mom a hug and kiss like he had been gone for weeks." *Mary*

"One of my earliest memories of Dad is our "dates" together. Dad would give me the choice of one roller coaster ride, one pony ride or gooney golf. Then we'd go out to lunch at the Chinese restaurant. On the way home, he always bought me a dozen Tyler roses. He also brought home a dozen roses for mom. These dates made me feel special." *Ann*

"I don't recall a time when Dad wasn't there for me. Every baseball game, every basketball game, and every other important event." *John*

"I love Grandpa because he says that I am "loving, caring, nice and beautiful and sweet." *Kristin*

"The greatest gift my parents gave me was their love and respect." *Mary*

14

Retirement

What fantasies come to mind when one contemplates the retirement years? For some, it is moving to a more temperate climate, or perhaps to a retirement community with its own recreational activities, or closer to the children. Or perhaps a move to a golfing community or closer to the beach. Occasionally foreign destinations receive serious consideration because of the low cost. Sadly for some it is to an assisted care facility especially one in which a person can advance to full nursing care. I don't think anyone completely escapes some of these thoughts but in Jeanne's and my mind, none of these were possibilities.

First, we love where we are. The climate has some shortcomings. Summers are long and can be very hot but air conditioning allows us to pick the temperature we like the best. Spring and fall are as delightful as anywhere in the country and winters are mild. The children live very close to us. The girls (Caryl, Ann and Mary) and their families live only 1 to 4 miles away here in the Woodlands. Joel III and Laurel live in Austin, a three hour drive, and John and Lisa live in Fort Worth, a four hour drive.

The grandchildren are more geographically scattered but the Bush Intercontinental Airport is nearby so we can travel anywhere in a few hours. All the family is very supportive of us and any illness brings the whole group to help in anything we cannot handle. Further, we have, literally, hundreds of close friends here with whom we frequently socialize and who are almost like family. The Woodlands has grown from a bedroom community of Houston to its own city and there is little to draw us away. We do still center our healthcare in the Houston Medical Center because it affords the highest quality care in the world. It is only a 40 minute drive away. We have been members of our church nearly 25 years so we are also firmly rooted there. It seems that there is nothing to attract us to other places to live out our final years.

I was not anxious to retire. I loved the practice of medicine. I considered it to be my true calling. I had received the finest of training and had been able to practice in an environment where the interest of the patient was paramount and health care was available to all. Then government and "third party payors" changed the landscape of medicine. It became necessary to see more patients in less time and to work longer hours to keep up with lower reimbursement rates and rapidly rising operating costs. At this point I longed to be able to slow down, and spend more time with Jeanne and the family. Private practice is very demanding and a patient's call for help interrupts anything one is engaged in or has plans to do.

Physically, I was doing all right. My prostate cancer seemed to be in remission and the side effects of the radiation treatment, though troublesome, were tolerable. Our partnership had recently added a new young physician (Donna Calabrese) who was as anxious for more work as I was for less. She was willing to take on my weekend call though I remained in the weekend rotation for taking care of hospitalized patients every fourth weekend. Night call was rarely a problem as the emergency room had full time emergency physician coverage.

I was surprised at how great a percentage of my income came from my weekend and night call duties. Still, I wanted to reduce my day schedule to four or even three days a week. When I put the pencil to it, I learned that the practice expenses would not go down, but in fact, would continue to rise as they had for years. I would be making too little to offset those expenses on a shortened weekly schedule, so if I wanted more time away from the practice I would have to retire. One of my former partners who had retired a couple of years earlier advised me to not retire *from* something but to retire *to* something. I understood fully what he meant. He knew that I would quickly tire of doing nothing productive.

The only thing to consider was what to do with my time. Jeanne was not retiring from her job as a homemaker or her involvement in church or community activities. Would I be able to help her so that her job would be easier, or would I be in the way? I wanted to do things with her and yet I did not want to smother her with too much togetherness.

I accepted a position on the Board of the John Cooper School, our local college prep school, where our granddaughter Elyse was already enrolled. Eventually five grandchildren attended this fine school. I am not sure how much I contributed to the board as it was not my area of expertise, but I did my best for six years. At the same time I became the unpaid medical director of a startup internet medical information company. We developed a fine product, better than some available today, but it failed financially despite considerable personal investment. Jeanne and I served together on the steering committee of the Retired Physicians Organization from the time of my retirement until her death. I was on the board of Alert Medical, a home respiratory therapy company, but resigned a few months later feeling they would be better served by a physician in active practice who would be dealing with the advancing technology and the problems of reimbursement.

Still another activity I carried into retirement was the John P. McGovern Museum of Health and Medical Science, known as The Health Museum. This had started in the early 1960's as an area within the Natural Science Museum. It received its initial funding from money left over after the massive polio vaccine program of 1962. Most of its maintenance funding in those years came from the Medical Auxiliary, now called the Alliance, and Jeanne served on the board of that organization. I began my service with The Health Museum as Chairman of the exhibits committee and became a member of the board, the program committee and the executive committee before my terms were over. Since then, I have remained on the advisory board.

Jeanne and I were both very active in church activities. I think that at one time or another we served on all the committees, many of them together and all the social ministries. Church really was like an extended family for us.

The other joy of our retirement was the Community Clinic. Dr. Joel Kerschenbaum, a family practitioner, started, in a storefront, a free clinic for the uninsured, staffed by volunteers and funded by private donations. What a marvelous thing for our county which had (and still has) a high uninsured population. As soon as I was able to solve the liability insurance obstacle, both Jeanne and I became regular volunteers. She felt that her nursing skills were outdated and worked as a receptionist and I saw patients in this wonderful setting with no insurance company's interference and no government regulation. All services were free and all volunteers unpaid. I still delight in working there. We now have a state of the art building paid for by private and foundation gifts. It is located right across the highway from The Woodlands Mall. The latest statistics (2008) show that the Clinic's 150 volunteers (physicians, physician assistants, nurses, social workers, receptionists, translators) provided 12,997 services with a value of over $1.5 million! What a delight to be able to provide care to those who would otherwise have no access to it. What a delight to work with these committed volunteers who are doing what Jesus referred to when he said, "When you do it to the least of these, my brethren, you do it also to me."

About a year after I retired, Jeanne was asked by the Retired Physicians Organization to provide a spouse's view of the psychological effects of retirement. This is the excellent speech she gave:

"RETIREMENT"
by Jeanne V. Reed

> I come to you today as an expert in the art of retirement. My experience is broad——one whole year.
>
> I have had varied experiences as a doctor's wife————- First as the wife of a medical student, then as the wife of an intern and resident————-Then a long tenure as an Air Force wife. Then we finally reached our goal. We were in private practice.
>
> All of this was very exciting and challenging. But none of this prepares you for retirement. Retirement was something we thought about in the far off future—in our dreams—mainly at times when life was very busy and we needed more quiet time together with our growing family. Retirement then looked very enticing.
>
> Years before, we had decided to move to The Woodlands. We thought it would be a nice place to retire years down the road. The Woodlands had a small town atmosphere and yet was close to Houston. That small town has more than doubled in size and population since we moved

there, proving once again that nothing stays the same, especially in the Houston area.

THEN BAM!!! Retirement was here. I was skeptical. Were we really ready for retirement? Were we really that old? Time hasn't gone by that fast!! Well, all I had to do was look in the mirror. The answer was yes. The hair was graying and there were those telltale wrinkles.

I was worried about Joel most of all. He has always been so active in medicine, his practice as well as the HCMS. I knew he would miss his patients and the camaraderie of you all. I was right; however, he doesn't miss the hassles.

But, he has found other areas willing to use his time and exuberance. He's on the board of a local prep school, financial secretary at church, chairman of the exhibits committee of the medical museum and is acting medical advisor for a new internet company. So, as you see, we are not sitting around looking at one another. And, as I've heard many of you say, there are not enough hours in the day to do all the things you want to do.

One thing we have been able to do is to make some of the longer trips that we had delayed making. We have always enjoyed travel. We have been able to take a course at Rice University, and attend an Elderhostel.

As for me, my life has not changed too much. The house is still here for me although the male chores get done much faster and I don't have to deal with workmen anymore. In fact, he's so busy that he has not been able to do his number one priority job which was to alphabetize my pantry and refrigerator! Truly, I think he has backed off of this job because I told him that he could also do the cooking.

Doctor Cohen said that you would want to hear some of the downside of retirement. Well, Joel sometimes does the grocery shopping for me and buys a lot on impulse. These shopping trips have to be scheduled right after a heavy lunch in order to save the food budget. I get a lot of calls to the garage to help him with a project. That is," if I am not busy," or to go to the hardware store to pick up a forgotten item, again "if I am not busy."

All in all, I've enjoyed having him home and I hope he feels the same. I thank God every day for this special time we have together.

Jeanne's speech was well received and I can echo much of what she said. I have treasured every minute of the time we have shared during these now 13 plus years that I have not had to set the alarm to head for the hospital or office before sunrise and arrive home after dark. I quit teasing her about alphabetizing the pantry and refrigerator when she told me that if I did then I could take over the cooking. We did, indeed, travel a lot. Even during the practice years we travelled whenever we could usually with the children along. They inherited the wanderlust as well.

I served on the ad hoc committee to establish the Academy of Life Long Learning at Montgomery College (now Lone Star College). This was a volunteer organization to give courses to seniors in the county, mostly taught by retired people with special skills or knowledge, sponsored and administered by the College of Continuing Education. It grew rapidly and is now a vibrant part of the College.

Looking back I can say that the real loves in retirement were those activities in which Jeanne and I could partner and work together. We made a good team.

15

Travel

Both Jeanne and I loved travel, and travel we did at every opportunity. Caryl and George gave us a world map with colored pins to keep a record of our travels; today it is covered with pins. The few places we missed were ones not very high on our priority list, and we were able to visit our favorites several times. Many of these trips were with some or all the children.

The countries we visited include England, Ireland, Scotland, Holland, Belgium, Germany, Austria, France, Italy, Spain, Portugal, Morocco, Greece, Turkey, Israel, Canada, Mexico, Grand Cayman, Jamaica, The Virgin Islands, The Azores, Honduras, Costa Rica, Panama, Belize, The Philippines, Taiwan, Japan, Singapore, Thailand, Vietnam, Malaysia, Australia, New Zealand, and China.

We also visited every one of the 50 United States plus Guam and Puerto Rico, and almost all the U.S. national parks. It might sound like we never stayed home, but remember, this was over a period of 60 years of marriage. With so many places to talk about, I could easily write a whole book about our travels, but I prefer to mention only a few of the most memorable trips.

Our first Europe trip in the early 1960s was one of those where each day was spent in another country. Really it was a "sampler" to decide where we wanted to return. We especially enjoyed getting away from the usual tourist traps and interacting with the local people. We always learned at least a few phrases in the language of the country we were in. This opened many doors. This was a fun trip but we were on the move so often and were herded through so many cathedrals and monuments that there was little time for immersion in the cultures.

Our first cruise was to the Greek Isles in 1970. We were able to follow some of the Apostle Paul's travels to Ephesus, Corinth, Rhodes and Athens. It was inspiring as the archeologists had uncovered and partially restored many of the sites referred to in the bible. We then went on to Israel where things were still very tense. It was only three years since the "Six Days War" and many sites were still surrounded by barbed wire and other areas marked as mine fields.

Because of this our travel was restricted to Jerusalem and Bethlehem for security. We vowed to come back when things were more peaceful. We did so 25 years later with a group from our church, led by our Pastor Charles Kindsvatter. This time we toured the entire country and I don't think we missed a thing. Again, the archeologists had done such a great job that there was no uncertainty as to the identification of the sites. This trip really brought the Bible alive. I found myself walking back and forth over sites where Christ had walked, the same stones being still there.

Jeanne's family on her mother's side had emigrated from Germany in 1882. Their home was a town called Offenbach-am-Glan. We wanted to make a special trip there to experience her roots. I could not find it on the map I had of Germany so I called the German Embassy. The person I spoke to had never heard of it, and insisted that I must mean Offenbach-am-Mein or Offenbach-am-Rheine. I assured him that I was right and he consulted his map. He could not find it. Fortunately a cousin of Jeanne's had been there and remembered that it was close to Bad Kreuznach. Following her directions, I stopped at a gas station in Bad Kreuznach and on the wall was local map showing Offenbach-am-Glan was only 40 km away. We were able to tour the church there and even review the baptismal records which recorded her grandfather's birth. The family name was Jung and it seemed everything in town was Jung-this or Jung-that.

In 1972 we took advantage of an offer from Texas Christian University, the college each of the children attended. It was a charter flight to England and one could go air fare only which was a terrific bargain, or participate in land tours. We decided that the whole family would go, including Jeanne's parents, all five of our children plus Jeanne and me (nine of us in all).

Jeanne and I wanted to rent a house in the Bavarian Alps and use that as a base for local touring. Jeanne's parents wanted to take the land tour. Caryl was to go with her college roommate and her mother on a tour of Austria. Joel III was to tour with a high school buddy with a Eurail pass to as many places as they could. Ann, Mary and John were to stay with us in Bavaria. We all spent a couple days in London and then went our separate ways.

We rented a van in Amsterdam and Jeanne and I, along with Ann, Mary and John, set off to Bavaria. All were to meet there at the end of their tours and before the charter flight back to Texas. We arrived late on a Sunday evening and were met by the caretaker. He instructed us in the operation of the house's appliances and the central heat. The only place we could eat that late on a Sunday was the local tavern. When we returned to the house, the caretaker was waiting for us at the door. He gave us the news that while we were eating, he received a call that Jeanne's mother had suddenly died in Grenoble, France. We had not even unpacked and got back in the van and headed for Grenoble. It was tragic. She was walking along the street and suddenly collapsed without saying a word. We suspected either a heart attack or pulmonary embolus. We made all the arrangements to bring her body back and this was not easy in a foreign country, especially since none of us could speak French.

Fortunately (brother-in-law) George's employer Hewlett-Packard had an office in Grenoble, and he arranged for the manager's secretary to help us as a translator and negotiator. We were unable to reach Caryl or Joel as their itineraries were flexible. So we just left word with the caretaker in Bavaria that they should return home on the charter as originally planned. We put Ann and Mary on the TCU tour that Jeanne's parents had been on so they would also return on the charter. Jeanne, her Dad, John, and I returned on the same plane as her mother's remains. What a mix-up. It all worked out well, though, as the other TCU folks on the tour looked out for Ann and Mary.

As soon as we arrived home, we went to the funeral home to make arrangements for her funeral. We commented to the funeral director that we expected that we would have to purchase another casket here as we had never seen the one we picked from a catalogue in France. His response was, "Wait till you see it. You may be pleasantly surprised." We were, as the casket was beautiful, solid wood with hand carved cross more beautiful than any available here. We still look back on that trip as a disaster but were pleased that her death was sudden with no suffering, and that she was having such a good time on the trip. We felt very uneasy leaving four children in Europe but we could not reach Caryl or Joel and we knew the group that Ann and Mary were with would look after them and contact us if there was any problem. It was a tragedy to lose Jeanne's mother, but a joy to remember what a good time she was having.

In keeping with our desire to mix with the local people, we took a tour of Germany and Italy in 1966 following the recommendation in a book titled "Europe on $5 a Day". (That alone tells how long ago it was.) Caryl was seventeen and was travelling with us. The hotels were modest, usually homes that had several bedrooms with the living room serving as the lobby or common area, and with a shared bath. We enjoyed these accommodations more than the four star hotels.

In Rome we were in a third floor walkup pensione. I had written ahead asking the concierge to arrange for a guide for us as we wanted to tour on our own. He informed us that, since it was the height of the tourist season, all the guides wanted busloads of tourists so the tips would be greater. However, he was off duty the next day and would be glad to guide us. I was very suspicious as I felt he would charge us an unreasonable amount. He took us everywhere including the Vatican Museum and a special side trip to the Olympic Stadium which had been built for the 1940 Olympics. (His father was a sculptor and had sculpted two of the statues there.)

When we got back to the hotel, I thanked him and asked what I could pay him. He refused saying that it had been his pleasure and would take nothing despite my insistence. To top that, the porter who carried our bags to the room offered in perfect English to guide us that evening. His English was so good because he had been in the British Army in WWII serving in India. I asked him how he had ended up in the British Army and he said, "You want to be with a winner." He asked if we would like to see a typical Italian small town rather than more monuments. We were delighted. He took us to his home town which was only forty miles outside of Rome, had tea in a local tavern, toured the local Garibaldi museum (we were the only visitors and were taken around by the Museum Director), were taken to see his farm and then to his house for dinner. His home was much like a

New York tenement, one light bulb hanging on its wire, and a porcelain table that looked like it had come from grandma's attic. His wife and daughter (also 17 years old) served us prosciutto and salad and coffee. By then it was getting late and I asked him for directions back to the hotel. He insisted on taking us back. When we arrived, I tried to pay him for everything and he refused also saying it was his pleasure. I gained a new respect for the Italian people and for their warm hearts and hospitality. There was nothing like that in the fancy hotels.

    To try to respond to his gracious generosity, we invited him and his family to dinner the next night and to take a tour of Tivoli where the Cardinal had built a mansion with many fountains, a beautiful place. Despite the fact that it was only a few miles from Rome, he and his family had never been there. You cannot experience that type of interaction in the tourist hotels. We sent pictures and gifts to them at Christmas.

    Jeanne and I both loved the water and many of our trips were designed to be on or near a beach. Jeanne learned to snorkel in the Bahamas and was so enthralled by it that on one occasion I simply could not get her to quit and she suffered such severe sunburn on her back that it was covered with blisters. We snorkeled together and when the boys were along I dived with them in such places as Grand Cayman, Honduras, Belize, Bahamas, Cozumel, Cancun, and the Great Barrier Reef in Australia.

    John was with us on a trip to Nassau (Bahamas) in July of 1978. We stayed in a hotel on Cable Beach in which there was a casino. There was a sign over the door that you had to be 18 years of age to enter and 21 years of age to gamble. Since it was only a few days before his 18th birthday we let John enter with us to watch, warning him that he might be asked to leave. We only stayed an hour or so because we had set a budget we would be willing to spend for a little entertainment. John watched intently and the next day we saw him reading a pamphlet titled "How to win at blackjack" while he was lying on the beach. I knew what was coming.

Surely enough, that evening our son asked if he could play blackjack. I reminded him of the 21 year old rule but he responded, "If they don't say anything?" I agreed that if he decided before he started just how much of his own money he would spend on a few minutes of entertainment I would not object. He decided on $20.00. He stood behind the players for nearly an hour and then slipped into a seat at the table. He was not challenged and I stood behind him praying for him to lose quickly. Thank goodness, if he got 21 the dealer got blackjack and so on. I think it took about 10 minutes for him to go broke. He never asked to play again and, to this day, I don't think he would gamble.

Cayman was our favorite destination and we visited it so many times, almost annually, that we were able to take all the children and most of the grandchildren there at least once. Our favorite spots were Smith's Cove and the cemetery reef where the beach is public and the snorkeling is in a protected reserve. It is so loaded with colorful fish we used to joke that you could almost walk on fish. Jeanne's favorite spot was the Sting Ray City. She loved feeding the rays and holding and petting them; I don't think we ever went to Cayman without visiting the Stingrays. Though we stayed in several places there, our favorite condominium was the Silver Sands, an older place not far from the cemetery reef. It was never crowded and had over 550 feet of beachfront.

At first, I resisted cruising, preferring to get to our destination quickly by air and have more time to spend there. Jeanne preferred to travel at a slower pace. As with almost everything in our life, she eventually won me over and I came to like cruising at least as much as she did after I learned to relax. We took several memorable cruises. I have already mentioned the first, to the Greek Isles and early Christian sites. It always remained our favorite and we hoped to do it again, but the conflict in the Middle East caused us to keep putting it off hoping for more peaceful times.

Each cruise had its special times but the transatlantic repositioning cruise from Florida to Barcelona was exceptional. Caryl and George went with us and we had two weeks together. We love each other so much and have such a good time when we are together. They had not been to Spain before so they rented a car in Barcelona and spent another week travelling around Spain. It is too bad that our jobs kept us at such a great distance.

Just five days after my retirement date of December 31, 1995, we embarked on a trip to Singapore and a cruise through Southeast Asia. On the flight to Singapore a passenger in the first class section had an apparent heart attack. Although there were several doctors on board they felt that I, as an internist, should be in charge. There was also an emergency flight nurse aboard who helped as well. The patient was unstable and there was nothing available for treatment except oxygen. It was to be at least 10 hours before we reached our first stop which was Hong Kong. I recommended (seconded by the flight nurse) that we find an earlier landing spot. We were two hours away from Anchorage so we diverted there. We were met by EMT's who took the patient to the hospital. This resulted in our being fourteen hours late in arriving in Singapore, so our time there was foreshortened before boarding our ship for the cruise. We visited several ports in Malaysia, Vietnam and Thailand, ending in Bangkok. We had a great time in Bangkok and returned via Hong Kong where we also spent a few days. Jeanne had always loved Hong Kong and this time we could enjoy it in luxury.

Another especially notable trip was the one to New Zealand and Australia with Jeanne's sister Caryl and George. They were living in Canada and arranged their flights so that we would arrive in Auckland about the same time. As it turned out, we were both changing planes in Honolulu at the same time as well. Since their flight was considered international and ours was not, they had to stay in the international area of the terminal separated by a glass wall from the other areas. Nevertheless, we found them and conversed by sign language through the wall. At the same time a group of Maoris were returning to New Zealand and were being given a send off by their friends. They were singing a goodbye in the Maori tongue and it was beautiful, one of the best memories of that part of the trip.

We did arrive at about the same time and spent a delightful week on the north island of New Zealand, then flew to Cairns, Australia. We spent another delightful week there visiting the rain forest, the outback and of course, the barrier reef. Jeanne's snorkeling venture was shortened because she had trouble with a leak in her snorkel mask. Finally, the crew loaned her another and she did get in some time viewing the beauty of that reef. When we got home, I found the problem; a tiny grain of coral sand had wedged itself in the valve, keeping it from closing completely. Sharing that time with Caryl and George was as special treat. We have always been very close, so much so that George and I refer to each other as brothers, not brothers-in-law.

The trip we made to China was also a high point. I had the opportunity to join with International Surgical Society which was going to give lectures at various hospitals in China. I prepared a talk on pulmonary problems associated with major surgery, then never got the chance to give the lecture. This was 1984, which was before very much of China was open to tourists. Some of the hotels we stayed in were rather primitive. Nevertheless, we visited Hong Kong, Guangzhou (Canton), Shanghai, Xian, Guilin (Li River), and Beijing. Caryl had given me a tape of Mandarin and by the time we took the trip, I had about a 200 word vocabulary with pronunciation adequate enough to be understood. It is remarkable how much you can do with so few words and how it opened up communication with the people.

Jeanne, of course, loved the children and with as little as a "Ni how" (hello) they would come up to her and smile. We quickly learned that Chinese food is quite different from what we were used to at our local Chinese restaurant. When we got home Jeanne said it was the first trip we ever took where we lost weight. We always wanted to go back, especially to Beijing, but the trip was just too far to consider when Jeanne's health began to fail.

There were many more trips but I believe the ones we spent with the children and grandchildren were the best. We offered each of the grandchildren a trip anywhere they wished to go (within reason) when they were confirmed in the church. They were to make the itinerary and choose the restaurants and all activities. In fact, they were to be the "boss." Jennifer was first and her choice was Washington, D.C. I think we visited all the important sites (of her choice) and her favorite was the Smithsonian Air and Space Museum. It even interested her more than Dorothy's red slippers from the movie "The Wizard of Oz". We visited all the major monuments, toured the White House, the National Art Museum, the halls of Congress, Arlington National Cemetery and more.

Leslie and Catherine were confirmed about the same time and wanted to go together to Grand Cayman. They had been there in the past and always wanted to return. We revisited all there was to see on the island and all their favorite eating places, but most of the time was spent on the beautiful seven mile beach snorkeling at the cemetery reef, Smith's Cove and Eden Rock.

Joel IV is a fisherman and he wanted to go somewhere to fish for tuna or sailfish. We chose Cozumel so that we could fish in the channel between Cozumel and Cancun. The timing was off for tuna but he landed several large dolphins, also called wahoo or mahi-mahi. They are a beautiful iridescent green color when first landed. We even took one to the hotel and they prepared it for our dinner; it was superb. He also hooked two large sailfish and got to wrestle with them for awhile watching them leap out of the water, but they eventually got away. Much of the non-fishing time was spent snorkeling and sightseeing.

Elyse wanted to go to Cayman where she had been twice before with Jeanne and me and her parents. She also loved the water and the stingrays. On one of our trips to the stingray city we dove about 12-15 feet bringing up live conch. The boat captain prepared fresh ceviche from the conch. If you have ever seen a conch out of its shell you know that it is ugly. Few would eat it, especially knowing it was raw—but didn't bother Elyse. She loved it. She had her hair braided and ate at all her favorite restaurants and even ate three desserts at the Sunday brunch at the Hyatt. Three desserts is a family joke. It relates to a lunch date I had with Jennifer when she was about 12 years old. After a full meal, the waiter brought over the dessert cart and she selected her favorite. I then asked her if she would like another to which she responded positively. As she finished the second I again asked her if she would like another. She looked and was about to pick a third when she thought for awhile and finally refused.

Elyse wanted to parasail so we went to the place on seven mile beach where the boat departed. As we signed her up we were informed that she was too light and another would have to go with her in a dual harness. Jeanne spoke up immediately volunteering to go along. (Remember that Jeanne is in her late 60's at this time.) She was fearless and granddaughter and grandmother had a great time together.

Eric was next and wanted to go to Universal Studios in Florida and also attend a golfing school. We designed the trip so that we first went to South Seas Resort on Captiva Island, Florida. The big thing there was riding the jet skis and parasailing. The timing was right as he was the only customer at the moment so they took him up to 1400 feet and let him stay up much longer than the usual flight. Then it was on to Orlando and Universal Studios where I think we walked a hundred miles going to every show and attraction over a few days. Jeanne was not up to the golf school so she flew home and Eric and I spent the next three days with morning lessons and afternoon golfing with the pro.

On the first day, I slipped and fell on a sloping bulkhead and tore my left vastus (large muscle in the thigh). Nevertheless, I was able to go on, limping and finish the full three days of lessons and play. As soon as I got home, I went to my Orthopedic Surgeon. He confirmed the tear and said he could fix it surgically. However, he warned that I would be in a cast for 6 weeks and need 6 months of physiotherapy. I would then be 10% better. I told him that it sounded like he was talking me out of the surgery and he replied "exactly." To this day Eric remains a good golfer and the tear doesn't slow me down at all.

Caroline and Kristin were also confirmed at about the same time and wanted to go to Paris together. There was a lot of political unrest at that time and there had been some plane hijackings so we felt uneasy taking them abroad. I asked them to

Travel

consider alternatives. They went upstairs and got on the computer for over an hour. When they came downstairs, they presented me with a "contract" for a trip to Maui, Hawaii, and it included a list of all the activities they wanted to do while there. Besides the beach and boogie board surfing, they wanted to sail on the America's Cup sailboat, snorkel and swim with the spinner dolphins, shop, whale watch, and bike down the volcano. (It is a 33 mile bike ride, almost all downhill but not quite.) While we were waiting as the van was loaded with the bikes, I overheard someone saying that "yesterday there was an old guy about 60 doing the ride."

I was 75 at the time and kept quiet about it for fear they might not let me go. We started at the top in 45 degree, clear weather. As we descended, we went through fog, then mist, then rain, then mist, then fog and finally the sky grew clear and sunny and hot. We gradually peeled off slickers, coats, and sweatshirts and dried off in the warmth before reaching our destination. I think the only thing on the girl's contract that we did not do was horseback ride in the mountains.

Ryan had heard about the new Disney development called California Land. It is adjacent to Disneyland, really an extension of the existing Disneyland but with a California theme. It included many exciting rides and attractions and our tickets covered both parks. This was his choice for his trip. We stayed at the Grand California Hotel right in the park. By getting special tickets we were able to arrive at an attraction at a specific time and go to the head of the line. This, of course, eliminated the long waits in line and allowed us to do many more things.

His favorite ride was the rollercoaster which makes two complete loops around Mickey Mouse's ears. (That puts one upside down twice.) We got in line and he expected Jeanne to step aside at the last minute but she surprised him and went along. He still remarks about how gutsy she was to do that at her age. We were able to go to an Angel's baseball game and also took a day at Universal Studios in Los Angeles.

Bryan and Alissa were also confirmed about the same time. They have always been closest of friends as well as cousins. Both are quite athletic and love the outdoors. As soon as we began talking about their trips they wanted to go together and both picked Montana. They had visited their great Aunt and Uncle, Caryl and George in Whitefish, Montana, before and really loved the mountains. We planned our trip to include a visit with Caryl and George and while there we went to Glacier National Park.

There was still a lot of snow in the higher elevations so we took sleds and really bundled up for the cold. Bryan and Alissa hiked way up the mountainside so that they could have a long sled race down the slope. I waited at the base and watched them climb slowly much higher than I was comfortable with. As they were coming down, I saw a mountain goat come out of some brush nearby, way too close to me for comfort. Just then the children arrived. I asked for one of the sleds to hold in front of us in case the goat charged. It did tip its head as if to show me the pointed horns. I had them stand behind me and for awhile just stood our ground, then slowly backed up. When we were outside of the goat's comfort zone, he slowly walked away.

After a couple days we headed off for Calgary. It was just the right season for the wild animals to be coming out of their winter hideaways. I think we saw every sort of animal of the region including getting very close (in the car) to two grizzly bears, a sow with her cub. We also saw deer, elk, moose, mountain sheep and goats, and many small animals. I teased them that the only thing they had not seen was the elephant. We laughed a lot about that. When we got back to Texas, they gave us a picture album full of memories and on the cover they had put pictures of the various animals we had seen and included a picture of an elephant. Calgary was great. We saw a glacier, rode the cable car to the highest peak, rafted, hiked and swam in the hotel's indoor heated pool.

Christian was not yet confirmed, in fact, the Jones' had moved to a Community Church (Baptist) but he was baptized by immersion there. Jeanne and I felt that qualified him for his trip as much as confirmation had for the others. He chose Disneyland as his destination, so we were off to Anaheim in 2005.

Our "package" included a hotel inside the park and character breakfasts in which Christian was able to shake hands and talk to the different Disney characters and pose for pictures with them. It also included 200 Disney Dollars which could be spent in any of the stores in the park. Of course, we let him decide what he wanted to buy. We were both amazed at how carefully he shopped, making no quick decisions, usually putting off a decision for a day or two, then going back to the store to decide.

His biggest and clearly the best purchase was a "bomber jacket" with many patches of various things on it. He wore it for a couple years till it just wouldn't fit anymore. I can't remember a single ride or attraction he didn't like, and there were many he rode repeatedly.

The wonderful thing about these trips with only one or two of the grandchildren at a time was the bonding experience. In this environment, away from any of the daily stresses and sibling rivalry, they flourished. Being the "boss" and being able to make all the decisions about where to go and what to eat and what to do made them feel somewhat older. Jeanne and I could focus on only one or two at a time and make them know how very special they were to us and how very much they were loved and respected as individuals. To this day each one of the grandchildren refers to themselves as our "favorite." I hope I can find the right words to make each one, children, grandchildren and great-grandchildren, know how deeply, intensely and genuinely we love and respect them as wonderful human beings, each a special individual.

16

Ninety Days

Does 90 days sound to you like a long or short time?

If you were waiting for a bonus check from your employer or for Christmas when you knew you would receive a long-wished for present, it might seem an eternity. Not so if it is your doctor's prognosis of how long you have left to live.

Except for the side effects of the first chemo-embolization treatment, Jeanne had remained fairly stable. She really didn't fear the second round of treatment which she had in early May. While she was still on the x-ray table, Dr. Roehm (who had performed Jeanne's procedure and who had put in my "birds nest" filter when I had my pulmonary emboli) came to me the waiting area. He said, "I want you to see the problem." I hoped he was just being extra nice because of our long relationship, going back to our days at Lackland Air Force base together. But the look on his face said otherwise.

"Problems?" I asked. He said yes. From the films it was apparent that Jeanne's cancer had spread and there were several lesions. He had treated the largest but could not treat them all. His advice was for us to see Dr. Ankoma-sey to see if there were any experimental treatments, since it was his opinion that the cancer was growing rapidly.

We arranged an appointment for as soon as possible. I believe it was only a couple days later. We both knew that there was no proven therapy available but hoped there would at least be something experimental in the pipeline. Dr. Ankoma-sey tried to present the grim news as gently as he could. He raised the possibility of referral to an oncologist but admitted on questioning that he knew of nothing with real promise. Jeanne wanted him to tell her how long she might have and we both had hopes of a year or two.

Prognosis is one of the most difficult tasks for any physician. Each patient is different and so many factors which are not controllable enter into the equation. Most physicians (myself included) prefer to answer questions about prognosis with statistics, such as 50% survive six months, and so on. This lets the patient identify with the longer survivors by doing a little math. But Jeanne was insistent that Dr. Ankoma-sey be specific, giving his best guess of just how long *she* had. He answered, "Perhaps 90 days. You should look into hospice care."

I don't think I can put into words what our feelings were at that moment. It still brings tears to my eyes whenever I think of it. It seemed as if the world stood still and the bottom dropped out. If we had been run over by a truck, it could not have hurt as much. We spent the next few days crying and holding each other before we could even talk about our next step. Granddaughter Catherine's wedding was scheduled for August, 89 days later. Jeanne's first thoughts were of that wedding. She determined that she was "going to make it to the wedding." She felt very close to Catherine and the feeling was mutual. We vowed that whatever was to come, we could face it together because we loved each other so very much, and that we would fully live what life was left to us.

We took the doctor's advice, at least partly, by calling our local hospice and meeting in our home with the hospice nurse. There was a lot of paper work, all of which we completed. But after looking at the details, we decided that we were not yet ready to discontinue some of the treatment that would have to be stopped to go into hospice. I asked her to keep the application on file as we were certain that the time would come in the not too distant future when we would take that step.

I searched the internet and the National Institutes of Health site, Medline, and clinical trials literature for other treatment options. There was nothing. I asked a friend who had many international medical friends to contact them to see if we could get into some hopeful research program. I called my ex-partner Harry Price, whom I felt was the best oncologist anywhere. He confirmed that there was nothing. Then he raised the possibility of a drug that was approved only for kidney cancer which had already spread (Nexavar). It was a drug which prevented the development of new blood vessels which were needed for the cancer to grow. Harry checked Jeanne over, did some lab work, and then gave us a prescription for the drug. I took it immediately to my pharmacist and waited while he processed the order. He came back in a few minutes and told me that my insurer (Humana) had denied the prescription and that I must file an appeal of their decision which could take weeks. It was an expensive drug costing about $5000 per month.

I felt we should start the medicine immediately and did not want to wait, so I told him to bypass the insurance company and get the medicine for me as if Jeanne was an uninsured patient. He called two suppliers who would not send the drug without the approval of the insurance company, even though I agreed to pay the full amount. He was about to call the third supplier when I said, "Let me call." I placed the call which was answered by a delightful young lady. I explained the situation to her and asked her to place the order as if it had come from a 35 year old patient with cash in hand..... even to say the request came from a foreign country if need be.

A long pause ensued while she discussed the request with her boss and when she returned she asked "When would you like me to send it?" I answered "Yesterday." She said she would send it overnight so that I would receive it the next day.

Nexavar had horrible side effects, but Jeanne tolerated them because it was her only hope to control the cancer. As time went by we were convinced that it slowed the cancer growth considerably.

We both wanted to buy as much good time as we could even though we knew that a cure was not to be expected. Most importantly, she desired to spend as much time as possible with the family, both children and the grandchildren, while she still had the strength to travel. We had taken a trip with Ann and family as soon as the ill effects of the first chemo-embolization had lessened. Ann was working as a school nurse and both Eric and Caroline were in college, so our first journey was scheduled to coincide with spring break so that we could all be together. Rick was able to get time off from his work at the same time. Our destination was Yosemite National Park and San Francisco. We rented a house within the park and thoroughly enjoyed the time together. Jeanne was not up to the hiking but kept up with all the sightseeing. She even went shopping in San Francisco with Caroline who helped her pick out several outfits which became her favorites in the coming months; in fact, she wore little else.

Our next trip was with Caryl and Al. Jeanne had always wanted to return to Paris as our previous visits there had always been with children along. Our activities on those visits had centered on what pleased the children and left little time for museums and historic sites. Caryl and Al wanted Paris to be special and a gift to Jeanne and me. They had visited there many times in conjunction with Al's work and knew all the special places. We began by flying to New York where Leslie, their daughter and our second granddaughter lived. Also living in New York was Catherine, our third granddaughter (Joel III's first child), and her new fiancé. We had a nice visit with them.

On the morning of sailing, we were treated to brunch at the Tavern on the Green in Central Park, a most luxurious and enjoyable meal. Then we boarded the Queen Mary II and headed for Southampton. It was a wonderful cruise and just right for Jeanne as there was plenty of time for rest. We arrived in Southampton, England, six days later.

Al had arranged for a limousine to take us directly to Gatwick Airport for our connection by air to Venice. All went smoothly but it was a very long walk from the air terminal to the water taxis in Venice for our ride to our hotel. It was still a few blocks from the taxi landing to the hotel but Jeanne did well. As you may know, in Venice there are no cars, so there is a lot of walking and every block or two there is a pedestrian bridge over the canals. We were only a few blocks from San Marco Square which is a center of activity. By short walks and water taxis we didn't miss much and thoroughly enjoyed this part of Italy we had never visited.

Then we traveled on to Paris where Al and Caryl had arranged a schedule fit for a queen—something we thought Jeanne was anyhow. He had reserved a particularly luxurious room—#614—on the top floor of the Hotel Regina with two balconies. These balconies overlooked the Tulleries and the Louvre which were both across the street. The view included the Eiffel Tower (She especially enjoyed the lights on the tower which sparkled every hour for ten minutes after 9:00 PM), the Arch de Triumphe, and Place de la Concorde and the Louvre.

Each day they had arranged for a luxury six-door Mercedes limousine and driver. Our driver was a handsome 6'3" black man from Martinique with sporty dark glasses and a blue tooth phone on his ear. He would carefully help Jeanne in and out of the car from her wheel chair. He always drove us right to the entrance of whatever site we were visiting. On Sunday we attended church service at Notre Dame cathedral. He pulled up very near the entrance, got out to get the wheel chair from the trunk and helped Jeanne into the chair. We noted that people were taking Jeanne's picture. I am sure they thought she was a celebrity so we told her to just wave like the Queen. It was worth a good laugh.

At the Eiffel Tower there was a line a couple blocks long but again he drove up to the closest point of entry and we wheeled Jeanne into line. Almost immediately an official came up and directed us to the head of the line where there was a wheelchair elevator. We were taken right in and visited all the floors viewing Paris from all angles. The same thing happened the next day at the Louvre.

The Louvre is built on many levels, even on the same floor but at each level change there was a wheel chair lift and an attendant to aid in operation. The French were way ahead of us on disabled access, and each attendant was kind and courteous. Because of that, we saw everything Jeanne had wanted to see with less effort than we expected. Next was the Mus'ee d'Orsay which was my favorite and I think Jeanne's also. We both loved impressionism and our preferred artist was Monet.

That evening we went to a boutique restaurant owned by a friend of Al and Caryl. The only tourists there were us. The menu was so extensive and purely French. The food was delicious and again, the service was fit for the Queen.

The next day Al rented a car equipped with GPS for the drive to Giverny (Monet's home). It was a most memorable experience. If you ever wondered where he got all those beautiful colors you would wonder no more after such a trip. They are all in the gardens surrounding his home. You can recognize scenes from some of his paintings. The Japanese bridge over the water lily pond, his front door, etc. After slowly walking through his gardens and photographing all the different flowers we, of course, went through the gift shop. Jeanne spotted a beautiful bouquet of silk flowers. I warned her that we couldn't pack them and would have to hand carry them all the way home. She really wanted them so we purchased them. It would be months later before I understood why she wanted them so much.

We then drove to Normandy. Al had stayed at an old French farm only 3 miles from the Omaha Beach and we had been able to find it using Google Global. By focusing in, Al could recognize the driveway, the several buildings, and the place where he had parked. I don't know how old the buildings were but they seemed to be very old, well maintained and though we were the only guests, the owner treated us like royalty. Our goal was to visit the beaches of the invasion of World War II and the museums adjacent to them. It was a very cold and windy day. Our first stop was Omaha beach, then Utah beach. These were the main points of landing for the American forces. I had served in the Navy during the war but spent most of that time in school (college) and starting medical school. I spent only four months at what was real wartime duty serving as a corpsman in the Naval Hospital at Bainbridge. I always felt guilty that many of my friends who also enlisted were assigned to units that saw combat, some not making it home.

As I walked the beaches, inspected the gun placements and imagined the almost impossible task that they faced, I broke out in tears and had difficulty stopping. A friend of many years was in the third wave of the invasion and still suffered nightmares. He said that there were so many dead that he literally walked on bodies and body parts before he reached the ridge that offered some protection. I also cried as I walked through the rows of grave markers at the beautiful cemetery just off of the beach. It helped somewhat when Jeanne and friends reminded me that I was where the Navy wanted me to be and that they could have given me orders elsewhere anytime they wished.

We then headed back to Paris for our last night before returning to Houston. Al had reserved rooms at the airport hotel so that we would be able to avoid travel through Paris in the early morning for our flight home. I had felt so chilled by the cold and wind at Normandy that I thought it was the cause of my shaking chills which began during dinner at the hotel. I excused myself planning to take a hot bath to stop the chill. Caryl got a thermometer and found that I had 103 degrees temperature. I had no localizing symptoms, no signs of a respiratory infection and no organ malfunction. My diagnosis related to the unpasteurized tasty cheese I had eaten so much of with my meals. It was local and I strongly suspected it was not pasteurized. For a time it did reverse the roles of patient and caretaker.

As the final part of Al and Caryl's gift to Jeanne (Paris) they had arranged for first class seats for the flight home. We didn't know until we were boarding the 747 when the flight attendant pointed for us to turn forward for our seats instead of toward the rear. What a life saver that turned out to be. My temp was down but I still felt terrible. Because of the first class, I was able to recline my seat all the way to make a bed and slept almost all the way home. It was a wonderful trip and it was a joy to spend the time with Al and Caryl.

Jeanne's next goal was to be able to go to Austin for Catherine's wedding. She was weak and the side effects of the Nexavar were very bad. We knew that it was the only medicine that had any hope at all of at least slowing down the growth of the cancer so Jeanne wanted to continue it. As time passed, we became convinced that it was indeed working. She had great difficulty eating so we tried all sorts of tricks to increase her caloric intake. High protein Smoothies and our own mixtures of milk, ice cream and various flavors helped.

She had ascites (collection of fluid in the abdomen) which had to be drained about every three weeks. As much as 5000 cc were withdrawn each time. The procedure itself was not unpleasant due to the skill of Scott Zela, Dr. Ankoma-sey's physician assistant. At the same time she was given I.V. fluids and albumen which always perked her up for the next couple weeks.

She was doing well enough that it was clear that she would make the wedding. Joel III rented the President Johnson room which adjoined the hotel ballroom where the reception would be held. Jeanne was able to travel by car, dress in her finest for the wedding and even lasted through the reception till the newlyweds drove off. She went to the room several times for a few minutes rest so that she could participate fully. When we returned home, her condition deteriorated. I was convinced that it was due to dehydration more than directly due to the cancer. I found a pharmacy which supplied nursing homes. I got all the equipment needed and with the help of a friend, who managed nursing homes, got a nurse to come and set up the I.V.'s.

Jeanne was what we call a hard stick, meaning there weren't any good veins and several sticks were usually needed to get the I.V. going. We gave her several liters of fluids over the next couple days. It was almost miraculous for she perked up in every way and began planning our next goal. Amazingly, each time her condition worsened, she would recover after another round of I.V.'s at home or in conjunction with withdrawal of the abdominal fluid, a procedure which was always accompanied by intravenous fluids and albumen.

We wanted to plan a trip with John, Lisa, Kristin and Alissa to the Grand Canyon but the elevations and the distance caused us to delay this and focus on events closer to home. Also, the girls' schedules that summer didn't allow it. I finally made the trip with them after Jeanne's death. Jeanne and I had both felt the Grand Canyon was one of the wonders of the world and we wanted them to experience it. I am sure that Jeanne was with us in spirit.

My birthday, October 10th, provided an opportunity to get the whole family together and Jeanne did so well with that we decided to plan Thanksgiving at our house which was traditional. Each of the families contributed part of the meal but it was all put together at our house. Again, she rose to the occasion despite what was obvious weakness. Being with the family always gave her spirits a boost.

By now we were thoroughly convinced that the Nexavar was working, not curing, but markedly slowing the cancer growth. We also did not discount the power of the determination which she had to reach these goals. We were long past the 90 days the doctor had predicted and felt that we could still plan for future events. She did well at Thanksgiving with lots of help from all the family. We had the traditional meal at our house, and soon after that Christmas became the next targeted goal. It was traditional to hold Christmas at our house, with dinner about 3:00 PM, then go to the early evening church service, then come home and open presents. She was very weak but participated in everything.

Jeanne's next goal was to be able to celebrate our 60th anniversary on December 29. Secretly the children planned an event fit for a queen. Everyone came including the grandchildren from New York, the grand- and great-grandchildren from Ohio, and Jeanne's sister and her husband George from Montana. They had arranged for a wine and cheese reception aboard the waterway taxi, cruising around the Woodlands Waterway, starting and ending at Flemings which is our fanciest restaurant. There we had a sumptuous dinner ending with a wedding cake with the same statuette that had been atop our original wedding cake, and on all the other family wedding cakes, as well. Again, Jeanne perked up and enjoyed every minute.

In spite of these wonderful events, it became obvious that we were approaching the terminal stage of the cancer. I knew how Jeanne was fighting to be with us all, not so much for herself, but she knew how her death would affect us so she tolerated the terrible side effects of the medications and periods of weakness and I am sure of pain, though she would never admit it. In one of the most difficult moments of my life, I talked to her and told her that when she reached the point at which she was ready to go, I would accept that decision as painful as it would be.

She still had one more goal she had to make. That was the senior ring ceremony of Eric and Elyse at Texas A&M. It is apparently very important to the students and of course, that meant it was very important to Jeanne. She had become so weak; she could only get out of bed and into a wheel chair with maximum help and then only for a short while. Nevertheless she wanted to go to College Station for the ceremony to honor both Eric and Elyse. I think that one reason this was so important to Jeanne is that she knew it would be as close to their graduation as she could get.

To make the trip, I rented a 14 passenger van and had two rows of seats removed. In their place, I put an air mattress and then several pillows and foam wedges to make a bed. With the children's help, we got her into the wheel chair and out to the van, then into the makeshift bed and off we went to College Station, a one and a half hour drive. I had hoped the bed with all the foam and pillows would be comfortable enough for her to sleep but that was not the case. We drove right up to the building and reversed the process getting her back into the wheel chair to go inside.

You cannot believe what the ceremony consisted of. The building was a large sports arena and there were several lines. A, B, C, here; D, E, F, there and so forth. You were to get in your appropriate line and advance slowly till you reached the desk. There your ring was presented to you with a few personal words, and it was over. BUT, it meant a lot to Eric and Elyse who were delighted that grandma could be there. We had intended to take them all out to dinner before returning to Houston but Jeanne asked if we could come straight home.

Jeanne was exhausted when we got home and went straight to bed. On her 82nd birthday a few days later she got into the wheel chair and made it to the table for the birthday song and one bite of cake. Then it was immediately back to bed where she remained until her death six days later. We did get her admitted to home hospice as she wanted to die at home in our bed. The two of us had made a pact, years earlier, that we would die in our home, in our own bed and with our loved ones at our side. Her mind remained clear to the very end and her last words, moments before death, were "I love you."

She died in my arms. I thank God for that, though it was the most difficult moment of my life. She had been there at my side when I thought I was dying from my massive pulmonary embolism in 1989 and I had vowed to be there for her. I pray that it made the transition easier for her. I am sure that the first words she heard after her death were "Well done, my good and faithful servant."

Now it is two years later, yet I still grieve intensely. She was my special angel, a perfect wife, mother, grandmother, great-grandmother and friend. She touched so many lives and left the world a much better place. I try to focus on the joy that she now rests in Heaven as our faith is so strong but oh, how I miss her.

Epilogue

What a full, happy and joyful life. Looking back, I can think of almost nothing that I would change. Yes, health problems were a major concern and if the clock could be turned back fifty years and have then the knowledge and medical tools we have now, there would have been considerable differences. Isn't that true of almost everyone? We must live in our times do what we can with the knowledge and tools of the time.

World War II disrupted so many lives and too many were killed or disabled. But for me, it made possible entry into my beloved profession, medicine, and that led me to meet the love of my life, Jeanne. What a team we were. Then another war, Korea, and instead of combat in Korea, I was sent to the Philippines and was able to have my family with me for all but three months. The training and experience I had in the Air Force prepared me for an unusually fulfilling career as a specialist in the major medical center of the world, Houston.

Retirement opened many new doors and challenges which we were able to do together, including travel to so much of the world.

Does it sound like there was someone "up there" looking out for us? Well, it wasn't someone "up there" but was something in everything we did or thought or planned. Yes, love was the driving force and was present in our daily lives. As you know now, I equate God with love and if you desire a God centered life, just follow the example of Jesus who set the pattern and your life will be just as full.

What a conflict of emotions death of a loved one brings. Joy in knowing that she has, in Paul's words, "run the race" and indeed, won the race. She has reached what we all hope for, unity with God in Heaven. I don't understand what Heaven is like but it was described by Jesus as Paradise. In Jeanne's own words before her death, "What more could I ask for?" She was able to die in her own bed surrounded by the family she loved so much and was able to say, only moments before she died, "I love you". I know the importance of being able to say that as I had a similar experience in 1989 when I felt that I was dying of a massive pulmonary embolism. As I was passing out, I said "I love you and the children". That gave a feeling of peace. Why can't I feel joyful all the time?

Death when one is "in Christ" should be the most joyous time of all. After all, we have known since the very moment of our birth that we will die someday.

Instead, we focus not upon the joy of the departed but upon our own feelings of loss, separation, and loneliness. I know that I feel that everything in life has turned upside down. We did everything together especially during these last thirteen years of retirement. Yes, 24 hours of every day, and now it is all different. I feel lonely even though I am surrounded by loved ones. I keep busy doing the things we did together but somehow it is different. There is a hollow feeling in my chest even at joyful times with family and friends.

Nevertheless, as I look back, what more could I ask for? And as I look forward, what joy is to come when we are reunited?

About the Author

Joel E. Reed, M.D. is a retired physician who specialized in internal medicine and pulmonary diseases. Though he dearly loved the practice of medicine his greatest joy came after retirement at the age of 70. It was then that he could spend more time with his beloved family and pursue many areas of community service,

www.ingramcontent.com/pod-product-compliance
Lightning Source LLC
Chambersburg PA
CBHW041351290426
44108CB00001B/6